LIBERTY IN THE
AGE OF TERROR

A. C. GRAYLING is Professor of Philosophy at Birkbeck College, University of London. He believes that philosophy should take an active and useful role in society. He is the author of many books including *The Meaning of Things*, *Among the Dead Cities*, *Towards the Light* and *Thinking of Answers*. He is a regular contributor to *The Times*, *Guardian*, *Financial Times*, *Independent on Sunday*, *Literary Review*, *New Scientist* and *Prospect*, and is a frequent and popular contributor to radio and television programmes, including *Newsnight*, *Today*, *In Our Time*, *Start the Week* and CNN news. He is a past chairman of June Fourth, a human rights group concerned with China, and is accredited to the United Nations Council on Human Rights by the International Humanist and Ethical Union. He has been involved in UN human rights initiatives, the World Economic Forum and its advisory group on relations between the West and the Islamic world, and has served on civil liberties groups on questions ranging from Drug Testing at Work to privacy and free speech.

LIBERTY IN THE AGE OF TERROR

A Defence of Civil Liberties and Enlightenment Values

A. C. GRAYLING

BLOOMSBURY

LONDON · BERLIN · NEW YORK · SYDNEY

First published in Great Britain 2009
This paperback edition published 2010

Copyright © A. C. Grayling 2009

A. C. Grayling has asserted his right, in accordance with the Copyright,
Designs and Patents Act, 1998, to be identifi ed as the author of this Work

The Human Rights Act is reproduced under the terms of
Crown Copyright Policy Guidance issued by HMSO

Bloomsbury Publishing Plc
36 Soho Square
London W1D 3QY

www.bloomsbury.com

Bloomsbury Publishing, London, New York and Berlin
A CIP catalogue record for this book is available from the British Library

ISBN 978 1 4088 0307 3

10 9 8 7 6 5 4 3

Typeset by Hewer Text UK Ltd, Edinburgh
Printed in Great Britain by Clays Limited, St Ives plc

For all our children

The means of defence against foreign danger historically have become the instruments of tyranny at home.

James Madison, Speech to the
Constitutional Convention

. . . how necessary it is at all times to watch against the attempted encroachment of power, and to prevent its running to excess.

Tom Paine, *The Rights of Man*

The fact is we are willing enough to praise freedom when she is safely tucked away in the past and cannot be a nuisance. In the present, amidst dangers whose outcome we cannot foresee, we get nervous about her, and admit censorship. Yet the past was once the present, the seventeenth century was once 'now', with an unknown future, and Milton, who lived in his 'now' as we do in ours, was willing to take risks.

E. M. Forster, 'The Tercentenary
of the *Areopagitica*' (1944)

CONTENTS

PART II: DEBATES

Preface

This is a book about the war over civil liberties being waged in Western democracies. Because of the real and perceived threats posed by terrorism, many Western governments have been changing laws and introducing new laws that reduce civil liberties and citizens' rights, in the hope of making their populations safer. This book is a reaction to this important development. More, it is a response to the fact that reducing civil liberties in the hope of increasing security is a mistake of crisis proportions, with 'crisis' being the right word: for it is not only terrorism by itself, but its conjunction with our responses to it, which threatens the real political catastrophe of the age. Whereas it is obvious what threat terrorism represents, the self-harm of inappropriate responses to terrorism is less obvious, more insidious, and in the long term greatly more damaging.

Liberty, equality, justice, free speech, tolerance, privacy, identity and hope are the themes of this book, and so also is the question of the nature of the enemies of these things, and the dangers this tense age poses to them both from within and without.

Part I explains and defends the ideas that lie at the heart of liberties and rights. Part II engages with writers who have contributed, positively or negatively, to debate about these and allied matters. The urgency of this debate grows as the months pass; if we survive climate change and economic disasters, it should not be to find ourselves living in illiberal and closed societies, having created them because we frightened ourselves into doing what the enemies of liberal societies try to do with their suicide bombs and hijacked planes.

Acknowledgements

Some of the material in what follows first appeared – and mainly in earlier draft form – in various newspapers and magazines, including the *Guardian*, *The Times*, *Index* and the *Independent*, and in *Prospect* magazine. I am grateful to the various editors of these journals for the opportunity to express and develop these views in their columns. The rest of the material is new. A significant part of the background to the arguments here is provided by my account of the development of conceptions of liberty in particular, and civil liberties and human rights in general, in *Towards the Light* (Bloomsbury, 2007). The historical background there, and the contemporary arguments here, form a whole. Somewhat more indirectly I would include the even longer historical story about ideas of the good in the Western tradition in my *What Is Good?* (Weidenfeld, 2001) for its close relevance to the more immediate arguments of the present book and its 2007 fellow.

I wish to thank Anthony Barnett, Jonathan Cooper, Helena Kennedy, Maya Lester, Henry Porter, Lizzie Rogers and Bill Swainson for various and valuable helps during the work that went into this book.

Foreword

The pressures being exerted on civil liberties in Western countries come from two directions. The main one, sketched in the Preface above, is the mistaken belief that the right way to defend society against terrorism and crime is to dismantle some aspects of civil liberties. Civil liberties exist to protect individuals against the arbitrary use of state power, and authorities in all countries and times have found themselves inconvenienced by civil liberties, one main reason being that they make the task of monitoring, arresting and prosecuting bad people more difficult. But there is a good reason why civil liberties make the work of the authorities more difficult in these respects: namely, to protect the great majority of people who are not bad. Think of a typical police state – say, former communist East Germany – where there was no regime of civil liberties to stop men in long leather coats knocking on doors at 2 a.m., and the disappearance without trace of the individuals thus woken. The full implications of this example are too obvious to need spelling out. What it shows is that the inconvenience of the authorities equals the freedom of the people, and is a price richly worth paying for all that matters to individual lives and aspirations.

The pressure on civil liberties currently being felt in Western societies comes from within; it is self-inflicted. But it is self-inflicted in response to another pressure, an external pressure. This external pressure is terrorism; and not just terrorism as such, but something of which terrorism is only the vanguard – namely, the intensification of opposition to liberal social values that various forms of radical conservatism always exert. In recent years this has been happening with greater insistence and sometimes, as in the case of more extreme forms of Islamist hostility towards contemporary Western society, with violence.

The ambition to return Western liberal societies to a less liberal and more controlled way of life, chiefly by means of a revival of religious observance, is a familiar one, and waxes and wanes with the pulse of moral fashion. Militant and sometimes violent fundamentalism is the sharp end of this, both in itself and in its effect of inflaming more modest opinion into greater activism.

Some of the most militant religious fundamentalists, knowing that they cannot realistically hope to overthrow liberal and democratic societies, nevertheless desire to punish them, and do so by acts of mass murder, the worst to date being 9/11 in the United States, the London Underground bombings, the Madrid train bombings, and the attacks in Mumbai. This, obviously, is unacceptable, but so too is the background atmosphere of more general reaction which it both promotes and feeds upon. It is not enough to combat terrorism, therefore. It is also necessary to defend the liberal dispensation that fundamentalism, reaction, and their militant expressions, by their nature oppose.

Of course terrorism is a serious threat, and has to be countered. But the first direction from which pressure on civil liberties comes is even more worrying, because the actors here are the governments and security apparatuses of the liberal democracies themselves. Threats from fundamentalists and their like, even violent ones, can be opposed in a straightforward manner. But when societies begin to self-harm, much more is at stake. Western governments have undertaken military adventures abroad in the name of improving security at home, and this carries a variety of risks to the health of the home polities, to say nothing of the harm, collateral and otherwise, to the areas of the world where that action is taken. But acting to reduce liberties in our own societies in the belief that this is the right way to respond to threats of terrorism, is a mistake of a different order. It is compounded by the fact that almost all Western governments are taking advantage of the misnamed 'War on Terror' to increase surveillance and control of society generally, so that – they say – they can prevent crime and catch criminals and illegal immigrants as well as terrorists, and so that they can police and monitor society more effectively.

This over-inclusive, ill-defined, broad-brush justification indicates that their aims, and the reasons for them, are *ad hoc* and not clearly thought out. And they can thereby undo in a single ill-considered act of legislation what centuries of hard endeavour won in the way of individual rights.

In taking this tack Western governments are in part aided, in part persuaded and encouraged, by the fact that technology is making it possible for them to do these things in a way hitherto inconceivable. Or rather: in a way that has been inconceivable since religious belief in a sleepless and watchful deity has ceased to be widespread; for remember that churches once persuaded their adherents that such a being maintained an unblinking surveillance of everyone all the time – which is what our contemporary Western governments seem to be trying now to imitate, even as these words are written, by means of ubiquitous CCTV cameras and the monitoring of mobile phone, email and internet traffic, bank account transactions and other privacy-invading and liberty-restricting initiatives.

Nothing so far said implies dismissing or even underestimating the problems posed by terrorism – and also by crime and illegal immigration. We can grant that terrorism and crime are serious threats, yet argue that the destruction of civil liberties is not the way to combat them. On the contrary: part of the right way to combat threats to the liberal order is to reassert and defend its values. Terrorists – as their very name suggests – seek to frighten their victims into self-repression, thus making their victims do their work for them, achieving what the terrorists' brand of religious or political orthodoxy would achieve if they could impose it. To reduce our own liberties in supposed self-defence is thus to hand the victory to the terrorists at no further cost to them.

But it is not just the terrorists to whom victory is thus conceded. It pleases conservatives, especially religious conservatives, and it pleases criminals, though for different reasons. The religious conservative sees opportunities in the monitoring and surveillance that restricts personal freedoms;

he dislikes too much personal autonomy, and is happy to
see the eye of the CCTV camera do the work of a deity's
eye. The criminal sees a huge entrepreneurial prospect in
the creation of precious new commodities such as identities,
privacy, and centrally collated personal data: identities to be
stolen, forged and exploited, privacies to be blackmailed, and
centrally kept personal data to be stolen and sold or hacked
into.

Thus the self-inflicted injuries to our civil liberties play
into the hands of the terrorist, the radical conservative, and
the criminal. Moreover, they do so at enormous cost. This is
a very expensive act of destructive folly. The money for all
the technologies required for this new and universal system
of surveillance and tracking must come eventually – how
cruel an irony – from the pockets of the very people thus
turned into the equivalent of suspects in their own streets and
homes.

These points relate to practicality, adverse consequences,
and cost. But of course the main, the central, the chief point
is one of principle: that the freedom of the individual is a
precious and hard-won value which these measures corrosively
attack. What a tragedy it is that in our modern day, politicians
and indeed the public at large are now numb to questions
of principle. At the time that the British Parliament was
debating the introduction of a universal biometric identity
card scheme, I wrote a pamphlet on behalf of the civil liberties
organisation, Liberty, for distribution to all Members of
Parliament. I received scores of emails from parliamentarians
agreeing with the case against identity cards, but saying (in
the case of governing party politicians) that they were forced

to vote for the government line against their consciences, and that in any case an argument of principle would persuade no one in government, and that the best chance of contesting the identity card scheme was on grounds of cost.

This kind of response is, alas, a mark of our times. But it does not mean that we should abandon the argument of principle: after all, it was on principle that the great struggle for civil liberties was waged in the first place, and a principle can only be overturned by another and better principle.

That our own governments are busy destroying civil liberties, and creating large new problems in the process, should dismay all who live in the West. But it is happening with too little awareness, too little discussion, and too little accountability. When the financial markets of the world collapse, discussion of every aspect of what it means and why it happened is endless, and governments spend billions to bail out the banks who caused the problem in the first place with nothing short of feckless greed. Arguably the irresponsibility and cupidity of people in the finance industry has done far more harm than terrorism. But an even greater collapse in the socio-political order of the rights, freedoms and autonomy of individuals is discussed only by a few, and almost always too late: the contrast is stark and telling.

What follows is a contribution to the cause of protecting our liberties; if it fails, it will be another record of the protest some of us made at their demise. We should not wish future men and women who have to fight all over again for liberty to think that we gave up the courageous work of centuries without a struggle.

PART I
DEFENDING LIBERTIES

These debates – about free speech, censorship, civil liberties and human rights, 'Western values', democracy – can seem merely abstract to those who live in safe countries during peaceful times. But history teaches the depressing lesson that such places and times are surprisingly rare, and when they exist, they are not guaranteed to last forever. In most places and times, in fact, people have to fight for their liberties. Eternal vigilance is the least of it; there has to be protest and action too.

I write these words in an advanced and wealthy Western liberal democracy where it should be a given that civil liberties are secure, and where they can be taken for granted so that people can devote their energies to other things: to their work and families, to education, to the refreshments of leisure, to participation in the conversation of society, sure that there are safeguards against undue interference by the state, to being prey to its interventions and prying, its monitoring and control, and any danger of arbitrary and unchallengeable use of its power. This latter, we had once believed, is typically the way of things only in police states and tyrannies. Yet I find, to my great dismay, that I am obliged to argue in defence of civil liberties in my own home country, once vaunted as an exemplar of a free society, and once prepared to accept great sacrifices in wartime to defend liberty against tyranny.

My home country is the United Kingdom. The claim that it was once a model of a country where private citizens could feel secure in rights and liberties is not an idle one, though as Voltaire remarked, this fact did not owe itself to the constitution of the country, but to the constitution of the people. In the absence of written protections for civil liberties it has been all too easy for governments to change laws or introduce new ones, and to take administrative action without challenge, which amount to fundamental changes in those rights and liberties, most of which had been traditional and implicit rather than secured in law.

And alas again, almost everything there is to deplore in the steady and gathering erosion of civil liberties currently taking place in Britain can be said too of other European states, and even of the United States of America, to which one might otherwise naturally turn as the home and champion of liberty. One might naturally turn to the United States in this regard especially because it has what the United Kingdom lacks, namely, a written constitution enshrining some of the basic liberties required for a people to be free. If United States government agencies can hold prisoners without trial, torture them, and use the evidence thus gained in prosecutions, eavesdrop on its people without notice or remedy, and much besides that in any other circumstances or places would count as acts of tyranny – and alas yet again, these things happened in the United States during the two consecutive administrations of President George W. Bush – then there is danger indeed to the civil liberties and human rights that Western polities have historically prided themselves on.

For a number of years I worked with a human rights organisation which undertook lobbying at both the Commission and the Sub-Commission on Human Rights (as they were then called) at the United Nations in Geneva. The group's principal concern was the People's Republic of China, a major and persistent violator of the rights of millions in its vast land empire. But concerns about such matters are indivisible,

and all human rights lobbyists in Geneva were kept aware by
fellow lobbyists, representing many other people and peoples,
of the heavy burden of suffering and wrong that oppresses all
quarters of our world. But I did not need the experience of
working alongside other NGO activists to learn this. I had
seen it first hand while growing up in Africa where racism and
colonial exploitation abounded, and while living in the Far
East, especially in China, where the great majority of ordinary
citizens live in effect as forced labourers in thought and deed.
Passbooks, identity cards as internal passports for navigating
the streets of one's own home town, absence of freedom of
speech and movement, lack of privacy, political impotence,
punishment for thinking differently from orthodoxy, arrest
without warrant and imprisonment without trial, absence of
redress against unjust treatment and police brutality, arbitrary
interference with liberty and property, rights absent or
diminished because of one's sex, sexuality, age or skin colour
– these I have seen at first hand, and I have had a brush or two
with the inexorable power of authority when protesting these
matters; brushes which, though in my own case very minor,
were chilling enough to drive home the need to be part of the
fight for the rights of man, wherever and whenever it needed
to be fought.

That battle has now to be waged in our own home
countries, even in the West where the rule of law, a degree
of political enfranchisement, and civil liberties, are in large
part respected, but which for various reasons – whether
bureaucratic in the interests of 'efficiency', or with the
putatively well-intentioned aim of promoting 'security' in
an age of terrorism – are nonetheless under threat of being

compromised, weakened, and even rescinded by intention or mistake.

If we cannot protect our liberties in the countries of the West, which are the world's better political and social dispensations, how are we ever to encourage their spread to those in the majority world who still suffer their lack? Where are citizens of less free countries to turn if in the major Western nations illiberal laws are being passed and new grand schemes of surveillance and control are being put forward by politicians: extensions of periods of detention without trial, surveillance and monitoring by means as various as CCTV cameras throughout public space, identity card schemes, communications intercepts, the creation of new crimes and redefinitions of old crimes – the list is long?

Part of the problem arises from the fact that governments think they have to be seen to be 'doing something' in the face of difficulties such as terrorism and crime, even if they know that some of the measures they take are largely cosmetic. Another part of the problem is born of the fact that if people are paid to be full-time legislators, that is what they must do in order to justify their salaries: they legislate – not a little of the resulting law being unnecessary or even such as to make things worse.

But the chief reason is that too much government is infected by the bureaucratic belief that another regulation, another prohibition, another gatekeeper provision, another document or questionnaire, another police power, another biometric data device, will solve problems.

As the chapters to come argue, dismantling civil liberties is not the solution to those problems. Those chapters seek to make the case for the free society, a society that exists for mature, independent adults with a variety of interests and goals, the vast majority of whom possess common sense and basic decency, who recognise and understand the need for shared resources and sensible regulation for the common good, but who do not want to be policed, spied upon or required to live their lives with passport or ID card in hand to move about their own towns and country.

What I argue for should not be misconstrued as a version of 'libertarianism', which is different from 'liberalism'. By 'libertarianism' I understand an outlook that promotes the kind of absence of regulation cherished by right-wing, small-government advocates who want not so much freedom as license to pursue their interests economically and politically without the inconvenience of too many obligations to think about others. I write as a 'liberal' in the European sense, that is, someone who places himself on the liberal left in political terms, meaning that I retain a commitment to ideals of social justice – a view with a number of definite public policy implications – my commitment to constitutionally entrenched liberties and rights is very much one that has, at heart, the interests of those on whose heads 'libertarians' might trample on their way to getting an outsize slice of the pie. Libertarianism in this sense is close to theoretical anarchism, and is in fact not especially friendly to ideas of rights, because rights are obstructions to the libertarian's desire that there should be as few restraints as possible on what he chooses to do. An advocate of civil liberties wishes to see everyone given a chance to choose and act, not just those with the advantage of strong wills or great wealth or power.

★   ★   ★

One thing needs to be disposed of straight away. It is the claim, aimed at dampening the ardour of defenders of civil liberties, that 'if you have nothing to hide you have nothing to fear' from new laws and regulations that give the authorities greater powers at the expense of individual citizens. The answer to this is – oh indeed? nothing to fear from legislation that reduces civil liberties and extends the power of the state to detain, inspect, question, collect personal information, intercept communications, and deploy new and more instruments of surveillance and monitoring such as CCTV cameras and identity cards? The assumption behind the 'if you have nothing to hide' claim is that the authorities will always be benign; will always reliably identify and interfere with genuinely bad people only; will never find themselves engaging in 'mission creep', with more and more uses to put their new powers and capabilities to; will not redefine crimes, nor redefine various behaviours or views now regarded as acceptable, to extend the range of things for which people can be placed under suspicion – and so considerably on. It is all or some of naive, lazy and irresponsible not to be maximally vigilant regarding civil liberties and human rights, because it is a given that the liberties of individuals are inconvenient for all states and their security services, and in countries where there are few if any restraints (think Soviet Union – or even today's Russia – and China) it is liberty which quickly and comprehensively suffers. Where an alert populace can use its liberties (such as free speech) to defend its liberties vigorously, the universal tendency of states to increase their policing powers can be resisted: but even in such countries as the US and UK it takes real effort to mount and maintain such resistance. Consequently it is not acceptable to rest content with the 'if you have nothing to hide' argument, for it is one of the most seductive self-betrayals of liberty one can imagine.

And one ought never to forget, either, that it is easier for governments to create laws and instruments that compromise civil liberties than for them to be repealed or moderated subsequently. Examples are legion; in Britain no one should be allowed to forget the debacle of the Official Secrets Act 1911, the infamous 'Section 2' of which caused seventy-eight years of mischief by being too vague and wide-ranging: it was passed by Parliament in a single day in response to a temporary panic about German encroachment on British interests in Africa.

Rights and liberties are indivisible. Among other things this means that if one is serious about them, one is serious about all of them in the various guises in which they are implicated in the world's business. The chapters that follow reflect the way that questions about rights and liberties arise in different contexts and places. I write about free speech, equality, justice, democracy, identity and privacy – and government encroachments on all of them. I write about assaults on liberty from terrorism and from the 'War on Terror' both. And (in Part II, entitled 'Debates') I engage directly with several of my contemporaries regarding their views on these and related matters, using my response to them to further explore these ideas.

Liberty and Terrorism

Every age has its pressing problems; at the top of the list for ours are climate change, the problem of energy supply, the negative effects of globalisation, the struggle for social justice, and – the question I address here – how we are to preserve our civil liberties while effectively combating terrorism. The conjunction of two things – the consistently high level of terrorist threat recognised by security agencies, and the persistent endeavour by major Western governments to introduce, as a response, ever more civil-liberty-compromising legislation – makes this an urgent question.

It is important to note some background to this dilemma. Even before terrorism became the prime justification for the draconian liberty-reducing measures under discussion here, Britain had become the most watched country in the world, with closed-circuit television cameras monitoring large areas of public space. When this measure was first rolled out there were no complaints; the cameras were regarded as doing – and more effectively – the job of policemen on the beat, and could be regarded as an enhancement of public safety.

But the combination of this near-ubiquitous monitoring of general public space with other measures has removed the initial presumption of benignity.

The 1994 CCTV-enabling legislation promoted by Conservative Home Secretary Michael Howard can be nominated as the moment when a conjunction of new technologies and a new attitude to policing and security began to take a grip. There were two sources of this development. One was a product of party political rivalry; the Conservative Party wished to distance itself further from the Labour Party by showing itself to be tough on crime, which they supposed to be an effective strategy because the traditional left-liberal consensus on home affairs matters had been 'soft'. However the Labour opposition responded, through its then shadow Home Secretary Tony Blair, by setting out an equally tough stall, to steal the Tory thunder. The who-is-tougher race that followed during the 1990s was one major factor in the second source of the change towards emphasising security over civil liberties: governments of both parties now sought to turn aspects of what had been temporary emergency measures to deal with IRA terrorism into permanent measures, justifying this on the grounds that terrorism had become global and more serious.

The fact that the emergency powers and special courts set up to deal with IRA terrorism had caused several major miscarriages of justice (one especially remembers the 'Birmingham Six' and 'Guildford Four' cases) was forgotten, at least by the public, as the new developments in security measures gathered pace.

But the conjunction of widespread CCTV monitoring with increasingly numerous and invasive further policies, not least the acceleration in introduction of these latter after 9/11, at last began to prompt anxieties across a wide constituency of people concerned about civil liberties. A series of criminal justice and anti-terrorism bills, the identity card scheme, collection and centralised storage by the authorities of citizens' personal data, and more – the relevant measures are set out in some detail in Appendix 1 below – have at last had the cumulative effect of stirring public alarm, and therefore opposition.

The change that has taken place in government thinking about civil liberties is a matter for great concern. For example: suggestions were made that microphones could be added to the nation's CCTV cameras to monitor conversations in the public spaces of British towns. As these words are being written, measures are before Parliament for dragnet collection of electronic communications data – information on the senders and addressees of every telephone call made and email sent by every citizen is to be passed to government and stored. New and extensive powers have already been taken by government for the security services to access citizens' private health, employment and banking records, and to eavesdrop on the content of communications directly.

The wholesale invasion of privacy represented by all these measures constitutes a massive change in the relationship between the citizen and the state, and turns the state into a snooper, a Big Brother institution, whose instruments of surveillance and control are premised on the idea that every citizen is a potential suspect, and must be treated as such.

To the motivations for these developments described above, and apart from the publicly stated ones of increasing security against terrorism and crime and combating illegal immigration, two more can be noted. One is the fact that governing political parties believe that they must be seen by voters to be doing everything possible to combat terrorism and crime, so that they can be re-elected. They see no votes in the statesman-like alternative of reminding the public that civil liberties are precious and that having them involves risks, and that security measures, though important, must not be allowed to compromise the long-fought-for and hard-won liberties that until very recently defined the modern Western world.

Moreover, full-time salaried legislators will fill their time with passing legislation that supports this aim of 'being seen to be doing everything possible' in the face of terrorism and crime: and the result will be laws that reduce civil liberties far more even than they are intended to do. For example: anti-terrorism legislation is now regularly used in Britain for such purposes as arresting demonstrators (two students reading aloud near Parliament the names of British military casualties in Iraq were arrested under this law), ejecting hecklers from party political meetings (a pensioner was removed under this law from a Labour Party conference for heckling the Prime Minister), freezing the assets of foreign banks (as in the case of branches of Icelandic banks during the 2008 credit crisis), and more. 'Mission creep' and the doctrine of unintended consequences are making the new security laws a catch-all for control and suppression unimaginable even a decade ago.

It has to be acknowledged – to repeat this essential point – that a principal driver of the new liberties-reducing measures is technology. The fact that electronic communications are wide open to monitoring and tracking – for just one example of the totality involved here: an individual can be located geographically by his mobile telephone signal, so not only what he is saying but where he is saying it is transparent to observers – has been the major factor in dismantling privacy, now virtually a thing of the past. The gathering, 'mining' and examination of data by computer, 'profiling' of travellers at airports, random visual and audio monitoring of the populace as it goes about its daily business, is all possible because of the already and growingly sophisticated equipment available to security services, their use licensed by government.

The biometric data identity card scheme is the classic example of how the new surveillance-state dispensation is being driven by technology – and by the commercial interests behind technology. The biometric data companies, seeing billions of pounds worth of revenue in the offing, have persuaded the British government that they can provide a universal identity card scheme in which fingerprints, DNA, and all personal details from address and employment data to health and bank information, can be instantly accessed by chip and reader device. The chip can be the size of a full-stop in this text (see the websites of the biometric data companies for this claim: all this information is in the pubic domain), and therefore if plastic cards are regarded as too insecure – easily lost, stolen or damaged, and forged well enough to fool some people some of the time – the full-stop-sized dot can be implanted under the skin of a wrist or in an ear lobe. I discuss this more fully later.

In the face of all this, what are we to say about the other great fact: the threat of terrorism? It can be granted that a small measure of scepticism is justified as to whether invocation of the terrorist threat is not sometimes a convenience for governments wishing to assert greater watchfulness over the public at large; as US Supreme Court Justice Thurgood Marshall once remarked, 'History teaches us that grave threats to liberty often come in times of urgency, when constitutional rights seem too extravagant to endure,' a sentiment he might have inferred from James Madison's telling remark, that 'The loss of liberty at home is to be charged to the provisions against danger, real or imagined, from abroad.' But it is prudent to acknowledge that there are mad and bad people out there, zealots, twisted idealists and fanatics, whose idea of activism is to murder as many of the hated Other as they can. We know this because we have seen it actually and horribly done. It is therefore possible that there are some contemptible people planning, as these words are written, to set off a 'dirty bomb' in the heart of a great city somewhere, planning and hoping to kill tens or hundreds of thousands, and to inflict a terrible wound on the surrounding society. What is one to do in the face of this kind of possibility, which is undoubtedly real?

Here is one answer. In a time of genuinely serious threat it is justified to place temporary and careful limits on certain civil liberties, if a good case can be made for doing so. But the stress lies on all the words involved: 'genuine', 'temporary', 'careful' and 'if a good case can be made for doing so'.

Assume that the threat is indeed serious. Then it would be justified for a government to institute a temporary and limited regime of emergency powers, temporary in the strict sense that they lapse after a specified number of months, and are renewable for a further period of months on advice provided, after examination of the need for their continuance, by more than one group of independent scrutineers – say, a panel of judges, and a select committee of legislators. The proposal to renew the powers should then be debated on the legislature floor, and voted upon. Renewal might occur every so often for a period of time; some powers might be found unnecessary and allowed to lapse after a while, and others adapted, on the same lapsing and renewable basis, as the nature of the threat evolves. Eventually the threat will dissipate, and the powers can then die a grateful and automatic death.

But they should never be made permanent, and never be allowed to stand without review for more than a specified number of months, or at most a year, at a time.

With the safeguard of periodic renewability on these terms, such aids to security as monitoring of financial transactions, use of intercept evidence in court, and longer periods of remand, can be temporarily justified given the threat posed by bad people with access to increasingly sophisticated means to carry out an intention of committing mass murder.

What is unacceptable is permanent reduction of civil liberties, as currently envisaged, and indeed enacted, by a number of Western governments (see Appendix 1). The premise that underlies such moves is the false proposition that security matters above all else. It matters all right: but not above liberty and justice. Those who care about the latter are unlikely to be persuaded that liberty and justice have had their day and that we must now take ourselves permanently hostage, thus in any case doing what terrorists are themselves bent on doing by breaking our society and remaking it closer to their hearts' desires.

If Western governments wish to forge consensus on the question of how to enhance security while protecting civil liberties, something along the lines of the above suggestion is surely right. What possible reason, in any case, could there be for making permanent reductions to civil liberties? The head of Britain's MI5 says that the terrorist threat might last a generation; a generation is a blink of an eye in historical terms. What purpose does a government think will be served by permanent limitations on liberties once the threat has passed? – unless the purpose in question is the convenience of governments even in unthreatening times: for governments are ever alert for ways to make managing – and policing – society easier in the face of pesky citizens who will insist on having minds of their own.

This last thought is among those that should always be present in contemplating what governments do on the civil liberty front, as a salutary reminder that today's benign and well-intentioned administrations are not going to last forever, and circumstances might give future administrations reason to make very different uses of the instruments of supervision and control that have been placed in their hands. This has already happened; anti-terrorism laws were no sooner passed in Britain than they were used for quite different and inappropriate purposes as the examples already cited show. That the laws in question could so readily be applied well beyond the scope of their original intended aim, and that they were even used to arrest a Member of Parliament (the conservative MP Damian Green) and search his office shows that they are suspect in their very nature, and inimical to the fabric of civil liberties. All the cases are matters of public record, and are perfect examples of the way that 'mission creep' affects all legislation, making bad legislation a particular nuisance and eventually a threat.

2

Compromising Liberty

The first casualty of government actions that reduce liberties is personal freedom. No government would openly claim that it was their intention to do this, except in strictly limited ways, but that is the effect of what they do 'in strictly limited ways', partly because there is never anything limited about a diminution of liberty – once a liberty has been eroded, it is less than it was: there is nothing limited about that – and partly because the 'doctrine of unintended effects' always applies, so that limitations follow in other directions too. A classic example is the plan to introduce biometric data identity cards for every citizen, linked to a central computer, accessible by government and security agencies on demand. Let us surmise that one of the putative aims of such a device of monitoring and tracking the population is to expose illegal immigrants, who would be supposed not to have access to criminally supplied identity cards that look good enough and work well enough for enough purposes to escape the vigilance of the law. When the countries from which immigrants come have grown richer and more peaceful and immigrants go home –

when, perhaps, we are exporting our own emigrants illegally to them – the identity cards will remain. To what end? To the policing, monitoring and surveillance of the country's legal citizens. Only then, perhaps, will it become obvious to the country's legal citizens that their status has changed from that of private citizen to potential suspect under perpetual scrutiny. If this last remark seems exaggerated, consider: each citizen will have been given the status of a motor vehicle, which carries a unique individuating number so that it can be tracked, identified and located at will by the authorities when they require to do so. This is precisely the effect of giving each citizen a bar code which instantly tells an agent of the authorities that individual's name, address, age, and, if required, a great deal of other information centrally collated from health, employment, financial and other records on a 'National Identity Register'. What this means for the privacy and autonomy of the individual, and the nature of the individual's relationship to the state, is surely clear.

An identity card scheme is one of the desires of the British government as these words are written. It was first formulated during the tenure of one of the most illiberal Home Secretaries Britain has seen, Mr David Blunkett, though it has since met so many practical and financial obstacles that its introduction has been delayed. But it is an example of what happens – so a sceptic will say – when governments remain in power too long: they exhibit an inevitable pattern, which is to run out of good ideas, and to fill the resulting void with not-so-good ideas. They also find themselves given to tokenism, seeking to be seen to be 'doing something' by passing laws in response to events, laws that too often are ill-defined and at risk therefore of being unworkable or counter-productive. This dismal eventuality has been coming to pass in major Western countries since the terrorist atrocities committed in the United States on 11 September 2001, and one of the chief features of the process is the accumulating legislation that encroaches on the personal liberty of individuals.

Of course, not everything that governments do in respect of legislation that circumscribes the liberties of some is bad. Arguably, what many critics think is a classic example of government meddling in private life, namely the ban on smoking in public spaces, adopted in several parts of Europe and the United States, is precisely not such an example. The ban was introduced for well-grounded health reasons, and far from outlawing smoking itself (which would indeed be a violation of personal freedom) it protects the increasing numbers of non-smokers from inhaling second-hand cigarette smoke, which after all consists of alveoli-damaging particulates to which the moist contents, including microbes and viruses, of other peoples' exhaled breath adhere.

The areas where legislation wrongly encroaches on personal freedom are thought, speech and privacy. Examples in Britain of efforts to compromise liberties in regard to speech and thought are the 'incitement to religious hatred' provisions of the Racial and Religious Hatred Act 2006, while the third – privacy – is deeply violated by the proposed biometric identity card scheme and laws permitting intercepts of all email and mobile phone communication. In the event, the attempt to limit free speech in the Racial and Religious Hatred Act was successfully restrained by a campaign of opposition.

Privacy is not just a matter of being left to get on with one's eccentricities behind one's own curtains. It is about each person having a space around his selfhood which he controls, not least information about himself that is no one's business but his own and those – doctor, bank manager, psychoanalyst – to whom he individually *chooses* to divulge part of it. The scheme to introduce, and eventually to make compulsory, identity cards for each citizen encoding biometric data about them, proposes to put vital personal information about individuals onto a central computer (in Britain the 'National Identity Register'), to be summoned onto a screen by government and policing agencies whenever they require. In the days when the phrase 'a man's home is his castle' meant something, it included this wider margin of privacy around a personal life; the identity card scheme tramples the walls of that castle down, and as noted makes each individual a number-plated conscript of the state, and thus puts him into a quite different relation to it; he or she is no longer a private citizen subscribing to membership of the state, but a chattel belonging to it.

Some will at this point say: so what? I would rather be safe than have this abstract difference you claim is made by not having an identity card or other 'liberty-restricting' measures in place. What is the fuss about? The explanation needed in response to this is: why liberty matters.

3

Why Liberty Matters

We tend to forget the value of things until they are lost, and personal freedom is a case in point. As we enter the zone long occupied by people in states governed by much more controlling and authoritarian regimes, we will come to think with regret of the principle we once thought we lived by: the principle of individual liberty, whose most eloquent advocate was John Stuart Mill.

In his classic *On Liberty* Mill argued that no government has a right to interfere with the personal freedom of individuals except to prevent them from harming others. Governments do not, he said, have a right to interfere with an individual's personal freedom even when they think it will be in his interests. If a government passed a law banning smoking (or, as the United States government did in the 1920s, drinking alcohol) on the grounds that it wished to protect smokers from harming themselves, it would be trespassing well beyond its limits.

Mill said that his aim in *On Liberty* was to assess 'the nature and limits of the power that can be legitimately exercised by society over the individual'. The reason why discussing this matter is so important, he said, is that one of the worst tyrannies that can be exercised over individuals is the tyranny of the majority. A civilised society is one that protects the freedom of individuals and minorities against majorities, just as it protects them against tyrants. 'There is a limit to the legitimate interference of collective opinion with individual independence,' he wrote, 'and to find that limit, and maintain it against encroachment, is as indispensable to a good condition of human affairs, as protection against political despotism.'

The reason for this, in turn, is that as long as human affairs are imperfect, the need remains for freedom of debate and opinion, so that a society can discuss with itself how to cope with its challenges and achieve progress. Equally, individuals need to be free to experiment with ways of living and seeking happiness, giving full scope to differences of character and choice, so long as they harm no one else in the process. For as Mill points out, where tradition governs how people live, instead of the dictates of their own characters and interests, one of the chief ingredients of human happiness and advancement is missing.

The idea that free development of individuality is essential to personal well-being, a thesis Mill always vigorously championed, is the key to why liberty matters. Conformist societies that frown on individuality are not merely repressive and reactionary, but stagnant. In every historical epoch distinguished by real progress in the arts, sciences and government, the prevailing social ethos has been an open one, hospitable to eccentricity, innovation, experimentation and the abandonment of traditions that have outlived their usefulness and become a barrier to progress.

Mill was writing at the height of Victorian conformism, in an era when middle-class self-satisfaction was at such full flood that the idea of too much individual liberty, and even more so the idea of experimental modes of life, was regarded with suspicion. This fact made Mill say that among his contemporaries individual spontaneity was undervalued, and no one felt anxiety about the boundary between social control (whether by means of moral coercion – the coercion of disapproval and ostracism – or law) and individual freedom itself. By the second half of the twentieth century, a century after Mill's time, in Europe and America the idea of individual freedom had trumped the constraints of conformism, a fact that played its part in the immense social changes that took place during that period.

But the mood has since begun to shift in the opposite direction once more, as shown by government efforts to shepherd social attitudes and behaviour by means of legislation. What can be the justification for this?

For politicians anxious to be seen to be responding appropriately to threats faced by the West from militant religious radicalism, giving up some aspects of individual freedom in return for increased security appears to be the obvious option. Evidently they have forgotten Benjamin Franklin's remark, that 'those who desire to give up freedom in order to gain security, will not have, nor do they deserve, either one'. This powerful and salutary observation should be inscribed on the walls of every government office. The reason is that liberty carries risks, and the courage to face the risks is what makes one worthy of having liberty.

Of course it is sensible to take precautions and to do one's best, while preserving one's central values, to guard against enemies. But there is a vital question here, of balancing liberties and protections in a mature society, erring always and greatly on the side of liberties. And there is an equally vital question of proportionality: if protective measures compromise freedoms, is the loss genuinely proportional to the risk? During the Second World War the British government introduced a series of security measures, including identity cards and restrictions on free speech, because an enemy army several hundred thousand strong was massing on the French coast twenty miles away, whose navy was assembling to ferry it across the Channel, and whose air force was attacking our own air defences daily. The measures introduced were *temporary*. Yet today our governments wish to introduce *permanent* and much-further-reaching measures, because a few dozen or a few score terrorists are planning atrocities, each one (to date anyway) smaller in scope than one Second World War bombing raid.

One of the signal events of recent years was the Danish cartoon outcry. The artificially inflated hysteria in the Muslim world, months after the cartoons were published, reveals a sharp division not between the West and Islam, but the West and radical Islamism. For the West (of which Islam is a part), free speech is the fundamental civil liberty without which there can be no others. Democracy requires debate and challenge, the rule of law requires the right to be heard in court, genuine education requires questioning and access to information. Without free speech none of these things is possible. Sometimes the price of free speech is offence, but 'feeling offended' can never justify censorship. Far more offensive than satirical cartoons, however poor in taste, are riots and embassy burnings, threats of murder and beheadings, an excessive and childish display by people most of whom have not seen or read the materials they have been told by their demagogues are 'offensive'.

Even here, though, reason governs. 'No one pretends that actions should be as free as opinions,' Mill wrote. 'On the contrary, even opinions lose their immunity, when the circumstances in which they are expressed are such as to constitute their expression a positive instigation to some mischievous act.' Think of the standard example: someone shouting 'Fire!' in a crowded theatre where there is no fire. One could argue that, in the tense climate of radicalism and terrorism, the Danish cartoons constitute just such a case; but equally one can say that the offence was not what was given, but what was (by deliberately provocative choice) taken. Anyone can incite themselves into feelings of outrage; why should this be allowed to silence others? One recalls the jingle, 'Sticks and stones can break my bones, but words will never harm me.' Although not literally true – words can indeed be harmful – the harm is not the harm of sticks and stones.

Western governments have not yet quite tried to redescribe words as sticks and stones because one minority group chooses to treat them as such, but they are coming close. So far it is the propensity to initiate action that remains the test of whether speech constitutes incitement. But a line has already been crossed: criminalising what people say, even with the best intentions for promoting social cohesion and equal respect, has to be rigorously limited if one of the most precious and important of all personal freedoms, essential to the health of society as Mill shows, is not to be compromised too far, and if something worth calling personal freedom is to remain.

As this shows, one of the main sources of danger to liberty comes from controversies that turn on 'feeling offended' by what others say or do, and using this as an excuse to limit their freedom to say or do it. And this in turn arises from the fetishisation of singular or overriding identities, almost always religious ones. As a contribution to understanding why liberty matters, one has to understand why questions of identity, and the politics of identity, constitute a threat to liberty.

4

Identity and Identities

In general it can be said that the fewer identities people acknowledge themselves as having, the less free they are. A classic case is religious identity: the more that individuals identify with their religion, and submit themselves to the way of life, relationships and routines it prescribes, the less individual, free and open they are. A monk or nun, a woman in a burqa, a priest with a large crucifix on his chest, present an overriding singular identity to the world, demanding thereby to be treated by others chiefly if not exclusively in terms of it. Leave aside the questionable fact that such people are thereby trying to dictate to others how those others should treat them – they are even indeed laying claim to a value that they expect others automatically to accord them – and consider this: our treatment of others of course does well to start on a basis of mutual respect, as invited by common humanity. But thereafter, how we relate to others should be determined by their worth as human individuals. This is not just a matter of thinking that the more diverse their identities the more interesting they are likely to be, as when one meets someone who recognises and acknowledges being all of a number of things – say: a mother, a medical professional, a tennis player, a writer, a member of a political party, a good friend, a daughter, all rolled into one – but who therefore has interests, experience and insights to offer that make her valuable to others in all sorts of ways. Such people live closer to the fulfilment of human potential, something denied or compromised by imprisonment in a single overriding identity, whether or not the imprisonment was imposed or chosen.

Thus, questions of identity have their place in the larger question of liberties, all the more so for being part of the current vexed changes occurring in Western countries where the settled values of the Enlightenment are under pressure from groups – some of them new: immigrants from Muslim countries have been at the forefront of this concern in such places as the Netherlands, for example – who want a share of the West's wealth but who do not accept its secular vision of what makes for the good in life. These are people who live by limited self-chosen identities, and who – if they were to win the argument – might kill the multi-identity goose that lays the golden eggs they came to collect.

At least part of the reason for the world's present discontents is that humanity is deeply divided within itself, mainly by chosen differences of ideology, religion, politics, and also by economic self-interest; not that these are wholly separate things. Race and ethnicity play their part too, but these are not matters of choice. When they are a source of division between people they are always made worse by political and religious differences. In our present world, it is the sharpness of a major religion-based divide which is – literally – drawing blood. And the religious divisions in question turn on using religious affiliation as the central feature of identity.

Even as the Berlin Wall was coming down in 1989, marking the end of the Cold War division between two ideological monoliths, some were predicting the approach of new and very differently motivated divisions. The best known is Samuel Huntington's 'clash of civilisations' thesis, to many borne out by the contemporary appearance of a collision between (to use the now-standard formula) 'Islam and the West'. It is no use objecting to this formula on the grounds that it opposes a religion to a geography; the terms are shorthand for two contrasting identities, two sets of values, two ways of looking at the world. And to that extent it refers to a real contrast – one has only to think simultaneously of the bikini on the Western beach and the burqa on the Muslim street to see immediately the sharp division that juxtaposing the terms 'Islam' and 'the West' can represent.

But not in all respects. There is far more wrong with the simplistic division into two identities than this last thought allows, which is precisely the point of an important essay on identity by the Nobel laureate, Amartya Sen.* His comments apply especially to religious identity, as the main motor driving today's increasingly bitter conflicts. Describing others, or thinking of oneself, in terms of 'a choiceless singularity of human identity' is the mistake and the danger which not only diminishes individuals, Sen says, but fuels the flames of conflict between them. His aim in opposition to this is to urge what should be the obvious-enough point made above,

---

* Amartya Sen, *Identity and Violence: The Illusion of Destiny* (W.W. Norton, 2006)

that a person is not one thing – a Muslim or a Jew only, or an Arab or an American only – but many things: a parent, a mathematician, a Bangladeshi, a man, a feminist, a Muslim, all of these things at once, and thus a multiple and overlapping complex being whom the politics of singular identity reduces to a mere cipher and crams into a pigeonhole.

These points are surely right, so it is all the more troubling that the tendency to overlook the many identities a human being has in favour of a single differentiating identity is on the increase. In fact this tendency has always existed, if less dramatically than it now appears, and was the norm before the days of 'political correctness' – which has a good side – taught us to avoid the errors of stereotyping on which racism, sexism and other forms of discrimination rest. But Sen is right to say that this tendency is animating more and more dangerous divisions as attitudes harden on all sides.

Sen's opposition to the politics of singular identity is not an attack on the movements whose followers adopt the identity that the movements offer. Can he separate the one from the other? He criticises the Huntington thesis, invoking the plural identities in past Islamic culture and the contributions it made to world culture, and cites Akbar, the sixteenth-century Mughal emperor, and Saladin, the prince of Islam in the twelfth century, as exemplars of pluralism and tolerance who gave house room to all faiths and persuasions. These are salutary points, aimed at helping to arrest the move towards greater divisiveness in a world that is now too small to contain it. But it overlooks the exclusivist claims made by these movements, and especially their fundamentalist wings, and the way that these distort human individuality into mere labels.

The unhappy truth is that the actors most responsible for insisting on singular identities at present are Islamist radicals. In contemporary Britain, for example, more and more young Muslim women are wearing the niqab – the face veil – as a political statement, asserting their Muslim identity as by far the most significant fact about themselves (indeed, given the nature of the apparel, the only fact about them) and in doing so forcing others to treat them accordingly. Whereas fundamentalist Christians in the United States might consider their faith commitment to be their main individuating characteristic, they are also Americans, Southerners (perhaps), businessmen, baseball or basketball fans, and (in many cases) Republicans. For an Islamist it appears that the religion and the politics are one and the same, and that little else matters in comparison. Overriding identities are the ones people are prepared to die for; in time of war soldiers are encouraged to make their identification with the homeland complete and their sacrifice for it glorious – this is precisely the use of singular identities that proves the idea's danger.

The main intended target for Sen's argument seems to be those in Western countries whose reaction to contemporary Islam, indiscriminately branded with the mark of Islamism, is to pigeonhole it simplistically. He does well to warn against this mistake, but of course he cannot withhold the charge against Islamists of themselves playing to the limit the politics of singular identity, and thus provoking this reaction. To them too the indictment of reductionism and a 'foggy perception of world history' applies, and with a vengeance whenever they use it as a *casus belli*.

A problem for debates of this kind is that they engage only those who read and think, and are unlikely to penetrate to the constituencies of ignorance and anger where their lessons are really needed. Because it is far easier for people to think in terms of singular identities, both for themselves and for those they already regard as enemies, persuading them to unlearn the habit is hard. Actual acquaintance with individuals – working with them, socialising with them – makes it difficult to think of them in group terms; but young men in the cities of Pakistan or Egypt watching Al Jazeera television are as far removed from that possibility as if they were on the moon – and the same for most watchers of television channels such as Fox News in America.

Worse still is the fact that some young Muslims of Pakistani descent in Britain, or Algerian descent in France, feel alienated from the mainstream culture around them, and grasp a singular Islamic identity as a shield and staff. In this lies the potential danger of identity thinking.

An eloquent voice that opposes the narrowing of identities by appeals to ethnicity, tribalism or religion is that of the Christian Lebanese Arab who is also a French citizen, Amin Maalouf, who says in his book *On Identity* (Harvill Press, 1998), 'As someone who proclaims every one of his allegiances from the rooftops, I can't help dreaming of the day when the region where I was born will follow the path I have described, leaving behind the era of tribes, of holy wars and of identities that kill, in order to build something in common. I dream of the day when I can call all of the

Middle East my homeland, as I now do Lebanon and France and Europe; the day when I can call all its sons, Muslim, Jewish and Christian, of all denominations and all origins, my compatriots.' Maalouf's principal suggestion is that, while retaining aspects of language and culture of their own, everyone should seek to 'identify to some degree with what he sees emerging in the world about him, instead of seeking refuge in an idealised past'. Amen to that.

Since the Second World War there has been a dramatically large rise (and it is still growing) in the numbers of people migrating to Western liberal democracies from less developed parts of the world, attracted by the wealth, openness, stability and opportunities that exist there. Despite the problems of racism and discrimination faced by many immigrants, enough official will to address them has existed in the host countries to make the chance of a decent life for immigrants more than merely a dream.

The different approaches countries have taken to the question of how to accommodate immigrants can be seen in the contrast between France and Britain. In France, the aspiration has been for everyone to be considered first and foremost French, with the eye of officialdom studiously blind to differences of ethnicity, creed and originating culture.

In Britain, the project of multiculturalism has been the preferred option, premised on the belief that a diverse and pluralistic society can achieve greater coherence through the recognition, acceptance and celebration of differences, allowing immigrants the space to preserve continuities of culture and belief as they see fit in their own communities.

For a while, both models seemed to work – at least to a plausible degree. But well before the beginning of the twenty-first century, both had begun to prompt serious doubts, and for the same reason: namely, anxieties in the host community that claims by immigrants (and, even more so, by their second- and third-generation descendants) to singular ethnic and religious identities were trumping any other form of allegiance to the host country, and any other commonality with the host population.

It seems that when an immigrant minority reaches a certain critical size in numbers while retaining or consciously fostering identity differences from the host nation, its political and social presence comes to be palpable, sometimes with the familiar and regrettable consequence of tensions and mutual hostilities between the host and immigrant communities. For example: in Britain minority religious groups have successfully acquired public funding for faith-based schools suited to their own communities, doing so by claiming equal entitlement with the tax-funded schools run by the host country's own Church. The prospects of segregation of children into religious ghettoes, given the extremely negative example of Northern Ireland in this respect, where segregation into Catholic and Protestant schools perennially kept community tensions at a high level, raise very understandable concerns. But so – quite rightly – does refusal to grant minority communities the same treatment as the host community.

'Identity politics' – and the uses, abuses, necessities and urgencies of religious identity – have accordingly become topics of serious debate, because they have disrupted the hopes of both the multiculturalist (British) and assimilationist

(French) styles of addressing the diversity introduced by immigration. If neither model has been proof against an insistence on singular identities – especially radical religious identities – as a tool or weapon in the hands of those who have come to repudiate their relationship with the broader society around them, what is to be done?

To critics of mass immigration, the appeal to identities derived from immigrants' cultures of origin is a symptom of the fact that immigration merely imports the underlying difficulties that had made the countries left behind so leavable in the first place. This is an analysis that is meant to explain why those among ethnic and religious minorities who currently 'play the identity card' are in fact second or subsequent generation British-born ethnic minorities, whereas their parents or grandparents (the actual immigrants) seemed, for a variety of reasons, to adapt more readily to their new circumstances.

The argument given is that a sense of alienation from the majority culture drives some ethnic minority Britons to insist on certain features of their originating culture as a crutch, prop, source of pride or affirmation, or as a barrier against indifference or hostility from sections of the majority population, with the effect of deepening the divide between them and exacerbating the problem. And this is fertile ground for trouble.

Such an argument overlooks the fact that the liberal democracies of Europe need immigrants, and therefore need to consider ways of welcoming them which avoid the difficulties and pitfalls that both assimilationism and multiculturalism have encountered. That requires a serious and thorough conversation. But another, associated, conversation must be had about the idea of identity itself, because if there is one lesson to be learned from the current insistence on defining identities (especially of a religious nature), it is that they have a great power to be divisive and provocative. That, of course, is precisely why some insist on them; but it is also why the politics of identity needs to be combated.

But while the salient aspect of the identity problem too readily associates itself in public debate not just with Islamism – the assertive political face of radical Islam – but with Islam itself, the appeal to identity is divisively at work in other contexts too: in nationalism in Scotland, for example – nationalism being just another form of identity politics writ large – and in the rise of a deeply unappealing English nationalism, which has too often been closely identified with racism, opposition to immigration and opposition to closer ties with the rest of Europe, and the expression of these attitudes in aggressive and sometimes violent ways. The underlying intention is to exclude, to divide, to raise and maintain barriers, even to excuse unacceptable treatment of others marked with a different label.

The mere thought of organisations committed to invoking ethnic, religious or national identities to explain, excuse, justify or promote attitudes and practices which divide people and promote conflict, ought to be enough to make us refuse to allow people to hide themselves or their purposes behind the disguise of an overriding singular identity.

The only identity that matters is that of being a human being – first, last and foremost. If that thought were in the

5

Equality and Justice

One major reason for the rise in identity politics is the lack of social justice in the world, a lack that expresses itself in 'them and us' terms where 'they' are in some way depriving 'us' of something we need or desire, oppressing 'us' in one of many ways, disrespecting something that 'we' value, or sometimes just doing better than 'us' for reasons that 'we' think are bad. These sentiments operate within and across societies; in both cases they are fertile ground for resentment and eventually conflict.

The concept of social justice is rich and complex. One thing that needs to be clarified in thinking about what it is – a necessary first step to considering how it might be achieved – is an idea that many think it turns upon: the idea of 'equality'. But it might be that an examination of the idea of equality shows that it is the wrong notion to serve at the heart of arguments for social justice, and that the concept of social justice itself – a concept of equity – is the right one. This, however, is harder to argue among those constituencies whose assumption of the armour of identity is their response to not having what others have; they aspire to equality of condition, whether by getting or being given what 'they' have, or by bringing 'them' down to 'our' level – perhaps by blowing up 'their' buildings, impoverishing 'them' and imprisoning 'them' in fear as 'we' might be imprisoned in dogma, ignorance, backwardness and resentment.

This is not to say that equality is an ideal without merit. On the contrary, it has great merit. A glance over the landscape of history shows that most grass-roots political movements are spurred by the ethical ideal of equality. 'When Adam dug and Eve span, who was then the gentleman?' asked the Levellers of seventeenth-century England, claiming primordial equality as the basis for human society. The same premise underlies the philosophy of Mo Zi in ancient China, the communism of primitive Christianity, and modern socialist and communist movements before the harsh realities of practice undermined them. Apart from them, the most famous movement for equality as a political goal in recent history was the French Revolution, whose aspiration to 'equality, liberty and fraternity' still resonates, although in the global success of capitalism it is only the second of these ideals that remains a slogan, applied more to markets, it seems, than individuals.

The modern egalitarian premise is not easy to state in a single sentence, for it has many formulations that capture its rich array of different senses. One possibility is: 'there is no inherent fact about any individual or group of individuals which gives them greater entitlements in any respect above any other individual or group'. This attempts to capture as generally as possible egalitarianism's opposition to formerly prevailing views about inherent differences between people and peoples: for example, that some people are 'nobly born' whereas others are 'base born', or that one 'race' is superior to another. And of course it also captures something that even past egalitarians might not have accepted; the equality of women and men.

But all attempts to define equality immediately run into problems. Are we talking about equality of opportunity, or political equality, or equality before the law, or equality of rights, or equality of income, or strict distributive equality in which each individual has exactly the same goods, benefits and resources as every other – or a permutation of some of these? Are all these kinds of equality equally valuable, desirable or necessary? For any one such equality, what is the basis of its being a value? Is it because equality in this or that respect promotes the cause of justice in society, or is justice quite different from equality? Could it be that justice is the real issue, and that equality as such is not very important at all – indeed, perhaps the wrong thing to be seeking? Talk of equality carries the assumption that all individuals and groups are equal in some respect or respects relevant to the kind of equality at stake – but what are those respects?

This last question has particular bite because, given how things are with people, history and the world, it is a hard fact that many different kinds of inequality exist at the starting point of any inquiry into the nature of equality, and any endeavour to bring about some form of it – not least the inequalities between the talents and natural endowments of individuals, and the luck affecting their life circumstances (such as being born in a rich country, or to educated parents).

These points show why the question 'equality between whom, in what respect, and why?' is vital from the outset. And this question in turn shows that the inequalities which prompt thinking about equality in the first place (inherent differences between individuals, the existence of unfairness and discrimination in social and economic arrangements, the skewed apportionment of the good things and opportunities of life, and the disproportionate allocation of power in society and the world) might not all be answered in the same way – and sometimes might not even involve equality as part of the answer.

Yet it is obvious that despite these questions, there is an irrefutable and insistent fact at the centre of our thinking about equality: racism, sexism, ageism and other forms of discrimination, in which one group of people is disadvantaged with respect to another on no morally, politically or legally defensible grounds, are unacceptable. When such discrimination occurs it has, among other effects, that of driving the victimised individuals into an identity group: the seed of division, sewn by discrimination, is watered by this reaction, and can scarcely help flourishing thereafter.

This means that a concept of equality as applied to individuals and groups in these crucial respects is a vital one, the application of which makes a large and palpable difference to the lives of those individuals and, one hopes in a non-divisive sense, the flourishing of those groups. Which concept of equality is this?

So the right way to start is indeed by recognising that claims of equality require specification of the respect in which two or more things are said to be equal. An old lady and a young athlete are not equal in their athletic prowess, their calorie intake, or their weight, but they are equal before the law, they are equally deserving of medical attention when needed, and they are equally entitled to the vote. They thus have social and political equality as citizens, whatever their other differences in age, sex, and the rest. So we would say: considered as little old lady and athlete, it does not matter that they need different calorie intakes; but considered as members of society, it matters greatly that they should be treated in exactly the same way before the law and in the polling booth.

For some, the differences between the lady and the athlete, and their equality as citizens, suggests that what really underlies the debate is fairness or equity, rather than equality. If the old lady and the athlete were required to consume exactly the same number of calories as each other – suppose that they have respective daily metabolic needs for 1,800 and 5,000 calories, but are obliged to consume exactly 3,400 calories a day each – then although they are being treated with scrupulous equality, they are both being treated unfairly; the old lady is being forced to each too much, the athlete too little. But if the athlete were given two votes and the old lady one, or if she were given special treatment in a court of law for the same crime as he commits, then that would be unfair or unjust as well as unequal.

'To each according to his needs' is one half of a famous prescription for justice or fairness; it is not a call for equality. One could accordingly reinterpret equality of rights and political equality as resting on a principle of justice, on the grounds that there is no sufficient reason for treating people

differently in these respects, as there is in the matter of
satisfying different calorie needs; and that to do so is therefore
unjust. By invoking the notion of justice, one answers
the question 'Why should people be treated equally (or
unequally, depending on the situation)?' This is one major
way that philosophers have sought to explain what equality
must mean.

It is an important way too, because it helps with a problem
already mentioned: individuals are not inherently equal in all
ways (talent and luck especially), yet morality demands that
they be accorded equal status in important political and social
respects, most especially in the matter of equal rights. This
latter idea has existed in different forms and traditions for a
long time (beginning in Stoic philosophy), but it received
its greatest recent impulse from the eighteenth-century
Enlightenment, which opposed the hitherto prevailing
assumption that individuals are naturally unequal, and not
only in talents and luck but in such supposedly inherent
qualities as 'noble blood', 'race' or sex. What first had to
change was the idea of justice, which then underwrote a
change in the way that human equality was perceived.

For the philosophers of classical antiquity, justice meant
'giving each his or her due'. If you were a member of an
'inferior' race or sex, your due was less than that of an
adult Greek male. If you were a woman or a 'barbarian',
and therefore had no vote or were less considerately treated
by the law courts, this did not mean that you were being
unjustly treated; it was simply not your due to be accorded
the same treatment in these respects as a Greek man.

The Enlightenment view is that everyone merits the same

dignity and respect as everyone else. This was the result of developments in the theory of natural rights and 'the social contract', based on the idea that in the state of nature everyone is equal, and that when people come together in mutually contracted social arrangements for the benefits this brings, they never fully forfeit their entitlement to self-determination and liberty. Famously, Rousseau argued that inequality in society results from the institution of property, which is not needed in the state of nature, and which is harmful once allowed, especially when the unequal distribution of property has become institutionalised and inherited down the generations.

The key to the Enlightenment's conception of equality is that it rests on the shared humanity of each individual as the appropriate basis for thinking about rights and entitlements. This is very different from assuming that there are inherited or intrinsic differences between people, which require us to discriminate positively or negatively between them. Once the default position is that each individual counts as one, considerations of justice require that they be treated equally in all respects other than when their needs or circumstances make it unjust to do so – as in the case of the old lady and the athlete.

Justice is itself a contested concept, of course, and there is much philosophical disagreement about its true nature. The idea of 'distributive justice', for a central example, raises questions about which social goods (and burdens) are to be distributed, to whom, and why – and what grounds exist for sometimes making unequal distributions, or exempting some from a share of the burdens. These questions follow from the question, 'In what respects should people be treated equally, and in what respects not?' – as exemplified yet again by our old lady and athlete.

A robust, common-sense outlook might be that at any point in the historical development of a society, there will always be a reachable consensus about what kinds of distribution of goods and burdens would count as just (or as fair) to all parties, including minorities. This is surely right. But at the same time it is hard to see how fundamental political and legal rights – such as the right to vote and the right to equal treatment before the law – could ever be differentially distributed in a society without this being unjust. This implies the existence of certain universal and inalienable rights, of exactly the kind that human rights instruments seek to protect. This too is surely right. So a society which recognises the claims of justice as the foundation of entitlement to equal treatment in one fundamental range of respects, and equitable (strictly fair) treatment in all other respects, is to that extent a good society. 'Equality, and where equality is unjust, equity' would be its appropriate slogan.

A way of dramatising these points is to say that a strictly egalitarian society would be unjust, and anyway unachievable, if it meant that unfair equalities prevailed. But this only reminds us that crucial equalities – such as equality of opportunity, equal rights and equality of citizenship status irrespective of age, ethnicity and sex – are the foundation of the just society, and are therefore non-negotiable.

That point is worth remembering when temptations arise to change some of these fundamental principles because we think that doing so would help in some emergency, for example in making a 'war on terrorism' easier to fight by making some people less equal before the law. In times of peace and prosperity, societies make grand gestures towards noble aims such as human rights and freedom of information, only to ratchet these back swiftly when hard times come. But these principles are precisely for the hard times: sticking by them is what makes a society truly just and worthy of respect.

An equal society might still be one in which different cultural interests existed and were cherished, each standing on the same footing as the others, though it is hard to imagine any individual or group themselves being serious about equality if a single or dominant identity mattered so much to them that they expected others to treat them differentially on the basis of it. Identity in this usual sense is thus a force against equality. Players of the identity card probably mean to achieve equity (fairness) rather than equality – for example, the same privileges and protections for their group as they perceive other groups to be granted by society.

But the hope has to be that an equitable society, a just society, will be one in which the need to assert an overriding identity as a way of making a claim on the consideration of others is lessened or even rendered unnecessary.

6

Civil Liberties in the West

I turn attention now to the way in which civil liberties and rights have been undermined in the United States and United Kingdom as a matter of policy. The governments of both countries claim to be promoting 'security' in reaction to the threat of terrorism, and in the UK the additional reason, somewhat haphazardly given, is that the same laws increasing the powers of the authorities will help in the fight against crime and illegal immigration. As this implies, boosting the surveillance, arrest and detention powers of security services, and reducing the rights of suspected persons, serve the interests of authority in ways that conveniently go well beyond the interests of security against terrorist attack.

There should be a special place for political irony in the catalogues of human folly. Starting a war 'to promote freedom and democracy' could in certain though rare circumstances be a justified act; but in the case of the second Gulf War that began in 2003, which involved reacting to criminals hiding in one country (Al-Qaeda in Afghanistan or Pakistan) by invading another country (Iraq), one of the main fronts has, dismayingly, turned out to be the home front, where the misnamed 'War on Terror' takes the form of a War on Civil Liberties in the spurious name of security. To defend 'freedom and democracy', Western governments attack and diminish freedom and democracy in their own countries. By this logic, someone will eventually have to invade the US and UK to restore freedom and democracy to them.

I say 'in the spurious name of security' because the degree of success of police action in the US and various European countries against terrorist plots prior to the passing of new legislation shows that terrorism can be combated within existing regimes of law, without having to diminish long-fought-for and hard-won civil liberties. But the US and the UK chip away at their own civil liberties, apparently indifferent to the consequences – and to the fact that they thereby do the terrorists' work for them, a point worth repeating because among the terrorists' reasons for seeking to hurt major Western countries is antipathy to the Western way of life: to their social and educational systems, their politics, their freedom of speech and belief, the freedom enjoyed by women, and other products of the individual liberty that defines them.

The first step in the Bush administration's war on civil liberties was the Patriot Act of 2001, a reaction to the atrocities of 9/11, passed just forty-three days after they occurred and with very little debate in Congress. (The Act is so called from the first letters of its full title: it is an Act to 'Provide Appropriate Tools Required to Intercept and Obstruct Terrorism'.) The Act sweepingly increased the powers of American security services. It licensed breaking into email and telephone communications and searching individuals' personal financial and medical (and library-borrowing!) records without a warrant, and without informing suspects that they were being investigated. It permitted wider intelligence-gathering activities abroad, gave summary powers to police and immigration officials to detain individuals indefinitely and deport them. It gave the US Treasury powers to examine and regulate a wider range of financial transactions, and redefined 'terrorism' to include many more activities (among them such 'domestic' crimes as those committed by the 'Unabomber', Ted Kaczynski, who over a period of eighteen years sent mail bombs that killed three people and injured twenty-two more) under this elastic term so that they would fall under the Act's provisions.

The Act provoked widespread opposition from civil liberties and human rights groups, and soon suffered setbacks in American courts as unconstitutional when challenged. For example, the detention of Brandon Mayfield and searches of his home because he was suspected of a connection with the Madrid train bombings of 2004, were judged to be violations of the Fourth Amendment when the matter came to court. More notably still, the American Civil Liberties Union took the FBI to court for conducting 'fishing expeditions' – looking through the personal health, financial and business records of tens of thousands of individuals unaware that they were under scrutiny, in the hope that something suspicious might appear – and it won the case, establishing that such 'fishing expeditions' using the Patriot Act violated the First and Fourth Amendments of the Constitution.

Originally a number of the Act's provisions were to have a 'sunset' four years after its passing unless re-voted. Among the permanent provisions were the security services' warrantless examination of communications and personal records. But President Bush's administration and its supporters on Capitol Hill pressed to have the entire Act made permanent, and in the event many of its controversial provisions became so in 2006, despite the protests of civil liberty organisations.

The Patriot Act was merely the first step. The kinds of powers it extended to security services were increased by other measures too, among them the Protect America Act of 2007, appositely renamed the 'Police America Act' by the American Civil Liberties Union. The new Act permits unrestricted and untargeted (in short: dragnet) collection of international communications without court order or proper checks either by Congress or a court of law. It gives only the scantiest protection for people in the US receiving an international phone call or email message, leaving decisions about the collection and use of Americans' private communications to the discretion of the government alone. It also licenses the US Attorney General, without any supervision by the courts, to give year-long warrants for surveillance of any individual he chooses.

If George Orwell were alive today he would recognise the Newspeak implicit in the redefinition of 'terrorism' to bring more and more activities under its net. Today's Islamist terrorists, properly so-called because their weapon is indiscriminate mass murder of civilian women, children and men, deserve condemnation as the worst kind of criminal. Drawing a line between 'security' and civil liberties is an exercise of real statesmanship and courageous recognition of the fact that freedom carries risks – very worthwhile risks. Bush's United States crossed that line in the wrong direction, and made the whole world a worse place by doing so.

But the US of course is not alone in doing so. Shortly after Mr Gordon Brown became Prime Minister of the United Kingdom in the autumn of 2007, he made a speech about civil liberties which received mixed notices: scepticism from some, an implicit challenge by others (including this writer) to live up to the better hints in it. A test for judgement of how Mr Brown's sentiments translate into action is provided by the fact that less than a year later he did everything in his power to see through the House of Commons a bill extending the period for which a suspect may be held without charge from an already grossly unacceptable twenty-eight days to forty-two days. Originally, for centuries (indeed, since at least 1215, the date of Magna Carta) no one could be held for more than forty-eight *hours* without the permission of a magistrate or the preferment of charges.

Not the least striking thing about Brown's civil liberties speech was that it was made at all. It displayed a consciousness that there is a constituency in his country, influential above its numbers, which is profoundly concerned by the effect of government policies on civil liberties. Compare that government's successive Home Secretaries to the greatest of Labour Home Secretaries, Roy Jenkins, a liberal reformer who ushered colour and fresh air into British society. Under Mr Blair, Brown's predecessor, there was the merest lip service to the 'British way of life' – meaning its liberal achievements in free speech, privacy, personal autonomy of the citizen, and the margin of individuality that all this implies – as defended (in characteristically generalised terms) by Blair in a speech made in Scotland, vigorously stating that terrorists would 'never make us change our way of life', when news reached him of the suicide bombing on the London Underground on 7 July 2005. But Blair's rhetoric proved empty because it was immediately followed by more civil-liberty-reducing security legislation (see Appendix 1).

This, one was inclined to hope, was not how things would be with Mr Brown; so major a speech on liberty was too big and emphatic a marker of intent, and at first it seemed that he meant what he said about honouring the tradition of liberty which in significant measure once defined British society. But some commentators immediately counselled caution in reaction to his speech, for by introducing the words 'and duties' as an annexe to 'rights', and by iterating the demands of the security problems we face, Brown left the door wide open for taking away more than he seemed to promise.

But if we took the positive aspects of Brown's speech at face value, they merited a constructive response from those who had been clamorous in print about the pressures that civil liberties were then under, as they still remain. And one important suggestion that could have been made is the one offered earlier in these pages: that in view of terrorist threats, some temporary legal adjustments might be endurable if they carried a sunset clause which makes them automatically fall at the end of a specified period, unless voted upon for further short periods. By this means certain supports to the security services during the time of maximum threat can be provided, but under periodic review, which means: under continuous recognition that they diminish liberties, that they are only temporarily justified by the needs of the hour, and are guaranteed to expire.

That would be a proper way forward. It would allow carefully circumscribed provisions, targeted at terrorist suspects only (and under a scrupulous definition of 'terrorist'), always with proper judicial overview as a safeguard.

But the attrition of civil liberties in the series of anti-terrorism and criminal justice laws that have followed hard upon one another in recent years have at last encouraged some (including this writer) to think afresh about the idea of a written constitution, the case for which has been growing rapidly stronger given the ways in which Britain's unwritten constitution has been degraded by these piecemeal, *ad hoc* measures in response to terrorism, immigration, crime, and new technologies. And a written constitution should at a minimum enshrine the principle that anything with negative implications for civil liberties – even merely possible ones – must carry default sunset clauses. Circumstances change; no polity should encumber itself with limitations and prohibitions permanently; the best safeguard for liberty is that anything questionable in light of it should only ever be temporary, if it must be enacted at all.

All the liberty-reducing measures and proposals mentioned here are serious enough; the risk to free speech, discussed next, does nothing but make matters greatly worse.

7

Free Speech and Censorship

Free speech is *the* fundamental civil liberty. Without it none of the others are possible, for none of the others can even be claimed or defended without it. That is one reason why there has to be a refusal to allow 'feeling offended' to serve as a license to censor the freedom to criticise and satirise.

'Taking offence' is a major technique of censorship employed especially by religious organisations and groups. Yet every religion, even the largest, is in a minority in the world at large; most people do not accept or share the sensitivities of any but one of them. If a religion is mature and self-confident, it should be able to bear with the disagreements, opposition, criticism and even ridicule of outsiders. The hysterical and disproportionate Muslim response to the Danish newspaper cartoons, for one example, suggests a profound lack of both those characteristics.

Social and political satire is one of the healthy features of debate in liberal democracies, and so is challenge and criticism. Efforts to silence people who say things you do not like to hear are regressive and unacceptable. Everyone who believes in a free, open and grown-up society should reject attempts to bully others into silence: free speech is simply too important to be compromised by anything other than the very best and most urgent of considerations.

So much is a statement of the obvious, or should be. It is remarkable that it needs to be said in the twenty-first century, and this very fact is a bad sign. All the more reason, then, to make the point, and to be clear about what it means.

There can be good reasons why information, or texts, or pictures, should be prevented from reaching the public domain by whatever agency has control of them, as when military and commercial plans are kept hidden from rivals. When this is a temporary expedient and reasonable in the circumstances, it is not censorship. Censorship proper occurs when (for example) a government or an organised lobby of some kind seeks to prohibit publication of information or opinion, or all or parts of texts or pictures, because it thinks its own or (often as a rationalisation) 'the public's' interests will be harmed by them.

A second and in many ways more insidious form of censorship is self-censorship, practised when a speaker or writer, or a body such as a newspaper or publishing house, voluntarily withholds expression because of fears of causing offence or inviting reprisals, whether in the form of a lawsuit or a terrorist attack. It is one thing for writers and publishers to oppose censorship of the first kind, but it is harder to resist silent decisions not to say anything about a controversial matter, or to omit reference to an inflammatory point. It might be thought that if censorship is forced by threats of violence, say, it is the threateners who are the censors;

some respond by arguing that both the threatener and the threatened share the fault, the latter in yielding to the threats by practising self-censorship.

Censorship and free speech must always be discussed together. One reason, the obvious one, is that the former is the denial of the latter, and as such is a threat to all other rights and liberties, all of which are fundamentally dependent on freedom of speech. This point is especially important and especially worth emphasising: I address it in the next chapter. What that argument shows, in short, is that without free speech civilisation itself shrinks and desiccates, and history attests to the stagnating effect of its absence: witness for example Torquemada's Inquisition in sixteenth-century Spain or the 'show trials' in the Soviet Union.

But a second reason is that there is a ticklish question to be answered concerning whether the right of free speech carries an obligation to exercise it. Do those who have the opportunity to speak freely have a duty not to impose censorship on themselves? This is a complex matter, because there is a difference between an author's right to say what he wants in his own way (under reasonable constraints to be discussed shortly), and his obligation not to self-censor for fear of offending someone, or of attracting reprisals, or to curry favour, or to avoid displeasing advertisers, and the like.

The possibility that there is a duty not to self-censor is suggested by the attitude of criticism which invariably greets the discovery of self-censorship. It seems timid at best, dishonest at worst. And yet there might be strong prudential reasons for doing it: for example, in the current climate of inflamed sensitivity on the part of some Muslims, publishing anything that can arouse their resentment, and therefore perhaps violence, gives pause for thought. On one hand there is the consideration that knowingly publishing something that might cause violence and even deaths is irresponsible. On the other hand, not publishing it is tantamount to yielding to the threat of violence, a capitulation that a free society cannot permit.

In this connection the right response is to identify the value at stake, and to consider how to defend it. For the reasons given below regarding its centrality to all other rights and liberties, free speech is a supreme value, and therefore both forms of censorship constitute a threat to the very structure of any society in which those rights and liberties are central. It follows that just as externally imposed censorship has to be emphatically contested, so self-censorship, even for prudential reasons, has to be emphatically repudiated likewise.

This is not to say that free speech is a wholly limitless right. There are circumstances – very few, and every time it is claimed that one such exists, a powerful case has to be made for saying so – in which, at a given moment in a given situation, exercising the right to free speech is irresponsible. The classic example is crying 'Fire!' in a crowded theatre when there is no fire. If someone did this in the middle of a dinner party it would merely be rude and inconsiderate; in the theatre it could be dangerous.

Printing satirical cartoons of the Prophet Muhammad in a newspaper has, given the circumstances in which it occurred, been likened to shouting 'Fire!' in a theatre. Is it? Here is the nub of the issue about self-censorship. Many are inclined to answer Yes, and if they are right, the self-censorship that quite a few writers, publishers and newspapers editors currently practise is vindicated. But the right answer is surely No, for the following reason.

Given that Western liberal democracies are premised on the rights and liberties for which free speech is essential, and given that free speech can only legitimately be limited on a case by case basis with exceptionally good reasons required each time, can it be acceptable to suppress free speech in the face of a standing situation, in which a sensitive minority wishes to be exempted from what all other figures and organisations are subjected to, namely criticism, satire, challenge, mockery, questioning, disagreement, even when some or all of these sometimes take scathing or hostile forms?

Put like this, a No answer is inevitable. In pluralistic and open societies the social conversation is quite rightly robust at times, because there are many different ways of making points and testing the credentials of those with claims, or pretensions, to one or another status. No one would dream of exempting politicians or political parties from such treatment, or trades unionists and unions. As civil society organisations of the same general kind, religious bodies have every right to put their case in public, and to work to further their interests, but they have no greater right in these respects than other civil society organisations, and – more to the present point – no greater immunity to criticism, challenge, or satirical attack.

The public debate can sometimes be ill-mannered and even tasteless, but neither is a reason for censorship. If censorship or self-censorship prevented any government or civil society organisation from receiving scrutiny, or if it was no longer possible to poke fun as one form of challenge, society would be in an unhealthy state. Censorship and the censorious always threaten to make it so.

On these grounds it is clear that the effort to censor the Danish cartoons by riots and violence, and by threats against the lives of cartoonists and editors, is infinitely the greater offence. It represents a crucial point of difference between the value of free speech and all that turns upon it, and the retrogressive, reactionary, static, punitive and mind-numbingly limited view that monolithic ideologies, spectacularly among them the more fundamentalist religions or versions of religions, seek to impose. The history of the last four hundred years is in large measure the history of efforts to assert the claims of liberty against just such monolithism. As free speech controversies show, the battle is still being fought.

In this chapter my aim has been to defend free speech even when it is offensive. The deep reasons why free speech matters are explored in the next chapter.

8

Free Speech and Civil Liberties

Liberty is not divisible; a society's members do not have it if they have only some of it in some spheres. That is why incremental reductions of aspects of civil liberty regimes are a danger: there quickly comes a point when the claim begins to ring hollow that members of a society have secure margins of freedom in their lives. The too-true cliché, endlessly worth repeating, is that the price of liberty is eternal vigilance, which is why it is mandatory to resist, and resist vigorously, the early stages of assaults on liberty, not least those made by well-meaning politicians who earnestly, eagerly, sincerely desire to protect us from bad people and from ourselves, for they are the most insidious agents of its destruction.

Yet though liberty is indivisible, regimes of liberties have a structure. The keystone of the arch is free speech. Consider what is required for people to be able to claim other liberties, or defend them when they are attacked. Consider what is required for a democratic process, which demands the statement and testing of policy proposals and party platforms, and the questioning of governments. Consider what is required for a due process at law, in which people can defend themselves against accusation, accuse wrongdoers who have harmed them, collect and examine evidence, make a case or refute one. Consider what is required for genuine education and research, enquiry, debate, exchange of information, challenges to falsehood, proposal and examination of opinion. Consider what is required for a free press, which although it always abuses its freedoms in the hunt for profit, is necessary with all its warts, as one of the two essential estates of a free society (the other being an independent judiciary). Consider what is required for a flourishing literature and theatre, and for innovation and experiment in any walk of life. In short and in sum, without free speech there is no freedom worth the name in other respects where freedom matters.

All this said, it is also true that there have to be limits to free speech at times. But it is absolutely vital that this be understood scrupulously and carefully, given what has just been said. What is shown by the standard example of crying 'Fire!' in a theatre or cinema is, obviously, the gratuitous causing of harm. (Actually, to say 'gratuitous' or 'irresponsible' adds nothing because there is no such thing as responsibly causing harm, as such; if harm is caused in achieving a greater good, as when one shouts 'Fire!' in a crowded theatre when there really is a fire, it is the undesired by-product of intending to achieve good.) Allowed too wide a reading, this can justify all manner of unjustifiable restrictions on free speech, as have occurred in liberal democracies in recent years (in the UK with the criminalisation of 'glorification of terrorism' and the criminalisation of 'incitement to religious hatred'). Restrictions on free speech have to be extremely narrow, extremely specific, case by case, one-off, and only very rarely, on the best justification, prior to the speech itself.

As the case of offensive free speech shows, the principle of freedom of speech promiscuously allows bad free speech, ranging from the stupid to the malicious and dangerous. If it is genuinely dangerous to life, as for example in direct incitement to murder, it invites a case-specific limitation. But generally the remedy for bad free speech is better free speech in response. In the case of libel and slander there is, as an instance of this, the remedy of the courts after the event. True, malicious mud-slinging is damaging even if a libel action is won, but free speech does not come free, and in a mature society we have to recognise that benefits carry costs, and this is one of them.

So vital is free speech to the health and liberty of a society that threats to it from whatever quarter and for whatever reason have to be challenged vigorously. Efforts to limit expression in Western liberal democracies are especially damaging, for they strike at the heart of what makes them both liberal and democracies. Censorship by coercion and special pleading is as big a threat to liberty in the West today as the actions by our own governments in diminishing our freedoms in the supposed interests of security. All who choose to come to live in a Western liberal democracy should be told that discrimination or insult directed at their age, ethnicity, disability if they have one, sex, and sexuality – the things they cannot choose but to have or be – will not be tolerated; but their opinions and beliefs, the matters over which they have choice, are open season for cartoonists, satirists, and all those who disagree: and they must like it or lump it, or if they are too immature or insecure, or both, to do either, they are free to leave.

All the above is directed mainly at the restrictions imposed on freedom of speech by our own governments in the last few years by security measures and anti-terrorism laws. A good example of how such laws violate important principles is the case of the misnamed 'lyrical terrorist', a Muslim girl who was prosecuted in Britain for writing poems in celebration of suicide bombers. This girl came to serve as an unfortunate example of the wrong-headedness of restrictions on speech. It is unpleasant to have to defend someone who glorifies mass murderers in a 'poem', yet consistency and principle demand it. Another example is the foolish mistake of banning a Dutch MP, Gert Wilders, from entering the UK to attend a showing of his film *Fitna,* which exposes Islamic radicalism. In this case, silencing Wilders by banning him amplified his message.

How far we have come from a time, worse in many ways than our own, when one of our judges could resoundingly say, as the eighteenth-century Lord Mansfield did, 'so long as an act remains in bare intention alone it is not punishable by our law'. That has changed, for example with conspiracy and allied laws (some introduced in another period of panic, the late eighteenth- and early nineteenth-century scare caused by the French Revolution), and now with the proscription of 'glorification' of such inglorious things as terrorism; and the British government has even sought to criminalise criticism of religion. The assault on free speech is well under way, which means – as the argument of this chapter implies – that the edifice of liberties is thereby threatened too.

Protecting a right to free speech carries the cost that some people are going to spout rubbish (perhaps 'most people' would be more accurate – look at the brave new world of blogging, in which some good sense is polluted by a great deal of nonsense) and some of that rubbish is going to be nasty – racist, homophobic, misogynistic, Holocaust-denying. The answer, suggested above, is to defeat bad free speech with good free speech, not to impose prior restraint on speech.

The right approach to bad free speech is to refute those who believe the world was created 6,000 years ago, refute the Holocaust-deniers and expose their agendas, argue down the racists and homophobes: in general, to challenge and defeat them with argument, not law. Law has its place in providing remedies in certain cases, most notably libel and defamation, but it is right that these are posterior restraints (kicks in the pants, so to say).

The reason for protecting free speech, even at the cost noted, is that it keeps bad views out in the open where they can be challenged, giving the arguments against them a full chance to be heard; and occasionally what is unpopular and unwelcome might be the right thing to argue for: think of the championing of gay rights in traditionalist societies today, where homosexuality is regarded with revulsion by moralisers.

Among the chief purveyors of bad free speech, as it happens, is the press. This raises interesting and significant questions about the press and its rights and duties.

Only in a free society is it a platitude to say that a free press is an indispensable mainstay of a free society. Like many platitudes it has the signal merit of being true. One can say more: that a free press, to be truly free, has to be allowed to take liberties so that liberty can be protected. But it should not therefore be above criticism, especially when the liberties in question do a disservice to the liberty in question.

A free press is needed all the more in a time of crisis like the present, when the public requires good information, careful analysis and perceptive comment to help it monitor the situation intelligently, and to assess the quality of their own government's actions in those circumstances. But as competition in the 24-hour media circus has grown fiercer, with desire for scoops replacing desire for the truth, the media has become a vehicle of sensation and novelty, which too often supplants news and analysis. That is another cost of the freedom accorded to the press; but it is hard to see how to do otherwise than bear it.

This is because, as the foregoing pages have insistently argued, free speech is so fundamental that there has to be extremely good reason ever to limit it. The First Amendment to the US Constitution forbids Congress to make any law that abridges the freedom of speech or the press; that is a safeguard which, despite everything, has repeatedly proved itself a bulwark of American civil liberties. It serves as an example of how the entrenching of the free speech principle makes it robust against the kind of attempted erosions of it that come from groups such as churches or religious movements seeking to limit others' free speech by claiming to 'feel offended' and the like.

The struggle for freedom of speech began in England when printing made the expression of views and opinions more difficult for authorities to control. The first prepublication licensing measure was introduced by royal proclamation in 1534, and succeeding governments made the restriction more severe while extending it from religious dissent to political opposition. The poet Milton famously attacked prior restraint of speech in his *Areopagitica* (1644), and his arguments eventually became a cornerstone of freedom of the press in England, and inspired the First Amendment right in the United States. But in England the free speech principle was not fully accepted until the principle in libel law that speaking the truth constituted a greater libel than spreading falsehoods ('the greater the truth the greater the libel') was abandoned in the mid-nineteenth century.

The long struggle to acquire freedom of speech is another reason for protecting it jealously in the face of persistent efforts by governments and special-interest groups to limit it. Grant that it has to be accepted that wholly unlimited free speech carries costs that are not always acceptable: speech that incites violence, or embodies or encourages discrimination on grounds of race, sex, age and disability, raises serious concerns, and there is clear justification for imposing restraints on it. But it is vital to be careful not to indulge in the careless thinking that sees this as a license to extend restrictions into areas where they are not justified – for a prime example once again: speech that criticises or mocks religious beliefs.

By far the best way of accommodating free speech is tolerance, to which I now turn.

9

Tolerance

One of the essentials of a good community – that is, a community in which each of us can build flourishing lives for ourselves and those we care about – is tolerance. Tolerance matters for the obvious reason that the diversity of interests and desires people have is sometimes so great that we don't even understand why others should think and behave as they do; and yet we acknowledge their right to do so, because we cherish the same right for ourselves.

Thus the very possibility of society turns on tolerance. Society involves people getting along peacefully all the time and co-operatively most of the time, and neither is possible unless people recognise the entitlement of others to their choices, and give them space accordingly.

But here, of course, is the familiar rub: the paradox of tolerance, which is that a tolerant society is always at risk of tolerating those who are intolerant, and allowing movements to grow which foster intolerance. The profoundly dismaying spectacle of today's Netherlands illustrates this point. What was one of the most inclusive and welcoming societies in

Europe has been stabbed in the heart by people it sheltered and who have grown into intolerant activists wishing to impose conformity and censorship on others by violence. And, alas, it has happened in the UK too.

The remedy for the paradox of tolerance is, of course, that tolerance must not tolerate intolerance if it is to protect itself. But this truism is often greeted with the response that if tolerance is intolerant of something, it is in breach of itself. The answer is to insist that although it is natural to think that tolerance is a warm, woolly, feel–good attitude, in fact it is a principle: it is an ethical demand that everyone should respect everyone else's rights and liberties. And this does the trick all by itself. Tolerance is not a demand to license just anything whatever, least of all behaviour that threatens the rights of others; it is a demand to respect others' rights and entitlements even when one does not agree with their views or share their interests. Tolerance thus has its central place in the good society along with other principles that stop it from being a merely flabby acceptance that anything goes. These are the principles of pluralism and individual liberty, which essentially require tolerance, but indicate its rational limit, which is: intolerance of anything that causes harm. Insisting on this vital point is what explains why tolerance not only cannot but must not tolerate intolerance.

It took the example of two centuries of the worst kind of intolerance – the kind that makes people kill one another – to produce in England a consensus on the need for tolerance in matters of religion. In his *Letter on Toleration* written in 1689, John Locke claimed to be astonished that anyone should seek to impose conformity of belief by force, though he was well aware that this was among the dangers to which the 'Glorious Revolution' of 1688 (in which he played a part) was a response.

Locke's feigned surprise that anyone should seek to coerce the opinions of others was a rhetorical device, its aim being to cement the relatively recently won consensus on freedom of conscience lest it should fray again. When Voltaire visited England nearly half a century later, he was able to admire the religious tolerance he found there – and the correlative lack of power of the clergy in state affairs.

Defending freedom of thought naturally and quickly led to the defence of freedom of the expression of thought. When Milton championed free speech in the seventeenth century he was ahead of the game; by the time William Blackstone famously defined freedom of the press as freedom from prior restraint (in his *Commentaries*, 1765–9) the principle was entrenched as part of Enlightenment thinking. The two ideas of tolerance and freedom of speech were thus entwined in the earliest stages of modern Western history, and the difficulties that both face in today's world are also intimately linked.

Both tolerance and free speech are fundamentals in an open society in which individual rights are respected and protected. Without free speech no other rights can be effective; as already noted, if one is silenced one cannot lay claim to any of one's other rights or seek remedies for abuse of them. But a society in which free speech is central is a society that must also be tolerant, because it will not infrequently happen that someone or other will be offended by someone else's utterances, this being an inevitable concomitant of free speech. Only if there is agreement both in principle and practice among members of the same society that they are prepared to tolerate opinions, sentiments, attitudes, and the expression of all three, that are different from their own, sometimes radically and even offensively different, can there be social cohesion and free speech at the same time.

It is important to notice that tolerance requires work. If people do not mind what others do, even when what those others do seems strange, alternative and remote, this is not tolerance; it is indifference (in the neutral sense that whether or not those others do it, the people in question are not bothered either way). But tolerance is an active thing. It involves recognising the right of others to be different from oneself, and allowing them the space and opportunity to speak from their different perspective and (under the usual constraint of not harming others) to live it out. It involves putting up with the fact that others seem odd, or offensive, or disagreeable. One might argue with them, try to persuade them to agree with or conform to one's own choices, criticise them, satirise them, and so forth – thus, exercising one's own freedom of speech in return – but not forbid or prevent them.

Of course, as we have seen, freedom of speech is not itself absolute, and toleration does not mean a limitless acceptance that anything goes. But freedom of speech is very nearly absolute; any limitations of it have to be specific, narrowly defined, and extremely well justified. And this means that the demand for tolerance is a genuine demand: it requires that people put up with a great deal of what they might not like at all, because the other party is entitled to say it.

The paradox of tolerance, and correlatively the great danger to free speech that comes from it, has already been mentioned. It is that tolerance allows too much margin to the intolerant. By defending the right of people to their opinions and the statement of them, we allow unsavoury opinions to flourish too, and to attract followers. We allow people who hate both free speech and tolerance to exploit our tolerance and perhaps eventually to overthrow our society and its liberties. This is similar to the anxiety people have about promoting democracy in countries where non-democratic ideologies are likely to triumph at the polls for historical reasons – just once. The fear of 'one man one vote one time' is what, for example, prompted the Algerian military to overturn the outcome of the 1991 elections in that country, which had given power to the Islamic Salvation Front (FIS).

The risk that tolerance will breed monsters is a real one, and yet it is a price that tolerance itself exacts, and has to be paid. This does not mean that our principles enfeeble us; the limit implied in the 'shouting "Fire" in the theatre' point is one guarantee that if free speech is abused by being an incitement to hatred or violence, there can be remedies. But society has to determine where the line is crossed from merely offensive to unacceptable speech. Is causing offence to religious sensibilities an example of abuse of free speech?

This of course is a highly current and contentious matter. As noted earlier, in 2006 the UK government sought, with only partial success, to place 'incitement to religious hatred' on a legal par with 'incitement to racial hatred'; this has played into the hands of religious minorities of various kinds in the UK who, in common with co-religionists elsewhere, have been quick to claim offence to their deepest religious sensibilities as a result of cartoons, theatrical productions and novels.

The answer to the question 'is causing offence to religious sensibilities an example of abuse of free speech?' has to be No. Placing restraints on offensive speech directed at people on the grounds of unavoidable facts about them is justified, as already noted, by the fact that people cannot change their sex, race or age. But given that a person's religious affiliation is ultimately a matter of choice, it is comparable to political affiliation, and obviously enough it would be wholly unacceptable to restrain criticism, attack, satire, mockery, scepticism, refutation, or anything else that might be conveyed by free speech in opposition to a political viewpoint.

Toleration thus turns out to have two dimensions. Tolerating the existence of others who have different views and ways of life does not mean that one cannot disagree with them or criticise them. Conversely, being tolerated carries with it an acceptance that one is going to have to tolerate the disagreement or criticism that comes at one from others. This applies as much to a majority host community being criticised by a minority immigrant community, for example over the racism or discrimination displayed towards them by the host community, as it does to the host community's objections to (say) the immigrant community's treatment of women, or its hostility to features of the host community's way of life.

This last point raises a different question about toleration. Is it intolerant to expect immigrant or visiting communities to respect the norms of the host society, and to live in reasonable conformity with them? Some answer Yes to the part of the question about *respecting* norms, and a qualified No to the part about *conforming to* those norms. This last amounts to the view that it is intolerant to require a degree of conformity to host society norms above bare observance of the law.

Western expatriates working in Saudi Arabia are careful to observe the restrictions on dress and alcohol consumption in force in that country. Recently there have been cases about the wearing of female Islamic headdress by teachers in British schools which raise questions of partial comparability: in this society it is regarded as undesirable for children to be unable to see their teachers' faces, just as it is regarded as undesirable for Western women to go out in public in Saudi Arabia with bare arms and legs. The comparability is not total, because the objection to teachers covering their faces in British schools is a pragmatic one, whereas the Saudi prohibition on limb-revealing clothing is one of conservative religious morality. The comparability enters when one asks, should Muslim women teachers in Britain seek to conform to British norms in this regard, as expatriate women do in Saudi Arabia? Or would they regard expatriate Western women living in Saudi Arabia as justified in asserting a cultural right to wear shorts and T-shirts in the street?

Saudi Arabian society is intolerant of Western dress and of many Western social practices, and there is a marked difference between the experience of expatriates living there and all kinds of expatriates and immigrants living in Western countries. In part the magnetic attraction of Western societies to immigrants, among opportunities for employment, education, health care and higher standards of life in general, is precisely their tolerance towards alternative viewpoints, manners, practices and personal choices. The asymmetry between historically tolerant and conservative countries is marked, and there is a large net flow of people from the latter to the former in consequence. The difficulty that some (generally, those hostile to immigration) perceive for the tolerant recipient societies is that immigrants will import with them the attitudes and practices which have made the countries they have left worth leaving. Unwelcoming attitudes to immigration are deepened and widened when the paradox of toleration begins to bite: again consider the Netherlands, until recently the most tolerant and open-armed of all European countries, which has been profoundly hurt by the actions of a small number of Islamists, whose intolerance for their host country has bred the beginnings of the same in return. This reprises what has happened in the United States, once the world's most welcoming and open-armed society, which has become vastly less so because of the Islamist terrorist atrocities of 9/11.

The difficulty, then, is for tolerant societies to preserve their tolerance and the free speech tradition which tolerance subserves, in the face of threats from two directions to undermine both. On one side are those hostile to the liberal outlook that tolerance makes possible: principally religious fundamentalists and the small minority of them who are also terrorists. On the other side are natives of tolerant societies who think that the route to security against terrorism is to make concessions to demands by religious fundamentalists who are intolerant of aspects of those societies, and to self-limit free speech and other civil liberties. This latter is happening to a dismaying extent in the UK (the biometric

identity card scheme, restrictions on free speech, plans for
detention for long periods without trial), the USA (Patriot
Act, Guantanamo Bay, and other reversals of due process and
civil liberty provisions), and other Western polities.

One way to limit free speech is by the 'chilling' effect of
monitoring it. The European Union is introducing measures
to increase the use of electronic surveillance, especially to
'harness the digital tsunami' as the EU Special Statewatch
puts it. The EU Council Presidency's own words are, 'Every
object the individual uses, every transaction they [sic] make
and almost everywhere they go will create a detailed digital
record. This will generate a wealth of information for public
security organisations, and create huge opportunities for
more effective and productive public security efforts.' Is this
the mark of a tolerant order?

There has to be a robust and sustained response to threats
to tolerance and free speech. One has to continue to argue
the case for them on every occasion of their being covertly
or overtly compromised, and one has to exercise them by
speaking out freely, and both giving and demanding tolerance.
Most of all there has to be an insistence that everyone accept
the fact that tolerating others and what they say can be hard
work – and not just accept it, but do the work itself. The
health and welfare of society depend on it.

The 'War on Terror'

The chief excuse for self-inflicted erosions of civil liberties in Western democracies is the real and the perceived threat of terrorism. The West's response to the terrorist threat has been to 'declare war' on it, and to use the idea of being 'at war' to justify a raft of laws and restrictions, too many of which are dangerous to civil liberties and therefore to the fabric of societies built upon their achievement. It is relevant now to turn attention to the question of terrorism and responses to it.

As an example of speaking truth to power there is little to beat criticisms of the phrase 'War on Terror'. Coined by President George W. Bush in the immediate aftermath of the 9/11 atrocities in New York and Washington, the phrase began as a rhetorical avowal of determination and became a policy, or perhaps it would be more accurate to say: a substitute for one. Critics are entirely right to challenge the phrase as vastly more harmful than helpful in the face of the world's present difficulties.

The first thing such critics are right about is the effect that the phrase has in lumping together all those non-state, self-constituted groups who choose violence as their means. A twofold problem results: one is that it offers the disparate groups a common identity, and with it a spurious justification to which they can therefore help themselves. Another is that it leads to a uniform approach being taken to dealing with those groups, when in fact each one requires its own tailored approach, in some if not many cases the most effective of which would certainly not be helicopter gunships and infantry battalions, or these alone. 'It is only the dullness of the eye,' said Walter Pater, 'which makes any two things seem alike.'

It is indisputable that whereas the hard power of bullets and bayonets can win battles, it is only soft power that can win wars, by fostering dispensations in which appropriate institutions and sustainable development can produce those two desiderata for all but the warrior-minded: peace and prosperity.

No doubt the very expressions 'soft power' and 'peace and prosperity' have too effete and soft-focus a ring for those who see the real enemy as Kalashnikov-bearing fanatics and suicide bombers. True enough, such people provoke the same reaction in many, who feel like shooting and bombing them in return, with an answering grimace of hatred such as they turn towards their targets. But they are actually symptoms of a variety of problems, not the whole of the problem itself. Terrorists are the pus in the festering sore, the flies on rotting offal. What caused the diseases that led them to cluster in the first place is a complex matter, rooted in history, exacerbated by humiliations and suspicions, inflamed by superstition, and made murderous by the availability of guns and bombs.

The situation we find ourselves in prompts more questions than answers. What are these causes of terrorism? Are they being addressed? What long-term plans are in place to provide the institutions, the social and economic development, the security framework, and the instruments of peaceful negotiation required to solve the problems that give rise to violence as the profoundly wrong would-be current solution, adopted by all sides? These are the questions to be insistently asked of those who have both the responsibility and the opportunity to answer them; but the first step has to be to describe the problem correctly, and to escape the distorting influence of rhetorical misdescriptions. If governments were disposed to listen to arguments about why it is a mistake to call the endeavour to respond to terrorism a 'War on Terror', it could be the start of a way out of the mire into which the whole combination of terrorism, its causes, and the response to it, has got us.

As a number of commentators, salient among them the journalist Thomas Friedman, have been rightly insistent in showing, part of the solution almost certainly lies in the allied problem of energy hunger. There is a direct relationship between the price of oil and tyranny in oil-producing countries – tyranny historically supported by other (mainly Western) countries hungry for the oil produced there. One way to get unstuck from the tar-baby of the world's most trouble-producing regions is therefore to find, and to find fast, alternatives to oil. It might seem remarkable to detached observers that this process, only just now beginning, did not happen after the dramatic and world-destabilising oil price rise of the early 1970s. But one has only to think of the oil wells, the fleets of ocean-going tankers, the refineries, the vast networks of distribution and the hundreds of thousands of petrol stations all over the world, to see what a weight of investment keeps the world at war; not just to sustain the oil companies' returns on their investment, but to keep turning the very wheels of economic life on which all – each one – of us depends. Thus considered, it would seem that the first urgency is to find other ways of powering our factories, homes, cars and lives, to free us from the place where a deeply unhappy mixture of fundamentalist religion and rich–poor power imbalances is as volatile and explosive as the substance it feeds on.

Is it any surprise that the other threat to the world, namely climate change, has something to do with the same promiscuous addiction to that same substance? It was a Faustian contract indeed, one that brought a double jeopardy, that made part of the world so rich, so flourishing, so hubristic – for so short a time after all – by dependence on the fossil remains of the distant past. Like drunks starting to sober up after a binge, and stumbling home through the dark, we see rats in the shadows, and feel the earth crumble beneath our feet: and both are the result of what we greedily consumed, without thought. So, one aspect of dealing with the sources of conflict in the world has to be identification of the oil nexus: energy hunger, the over-reliance on oil, the social and political problems of major oil-producing countries in the Middle East, the fact that some of the money Westerners pay for their petrol goes to the terrorists who attack them. Breaking this series of connections is part, but an urgent one, of creating a solution.

One alternative phrase that might be coined to replace 'War on Terror' therefore could be 'peace-making on the various problems part of whose outcome is terrorism'. Infinitely less glib and quotable than what it replaces, it at least has the merit of being more constructive, and wider in its reach over what has reduced the world to the primitive resource of bare-knuckle fighting as a supposed remedy for its turmoils.

And yet: terrorism occurs, taking the form of indiscriminate and wanton mass murder of women, children and men. It is a disgraceful and contemptible form of activism, perpetrated by people who have chosen criminal means to further their ends. It is indefensible, and has to be contested while different means are applied to dealing with its motives. The question is: how? And moreover, how, without damaging our own free societies in the process? To this difficult question I turn attention in the next chapter.

11

Combating Terrorism

It could be argued that, as the struggle against terrorism continues, one of the essential preliminaries for people in Western liberal democracies to understand, and for their governments to emphasise, is that this is not a war between the West and Islam. One reason is that it is not just the West whose civilian populations and economies have to be defended from attack by terrorism, for there are states in the developing world under the same threat from sections of their own populations who employ the same means, and whose support comes from the same dark spiderweb of funding and arms supply which links disparate terrorist organisations across the world. India and Indonesia, Iraq and Afghanistan, even Saudi Arabia, all suffer acts of terrorism, and although religion and religious differences play a leading part as both historical and contemporary factors, other factors, including of course political ones, contribute also.

But a more important reason for not casting these difficulties as a 'West–Islam' war is that the majority of Muslims – as the moderate voices among them are keen to claim – are peaceful and generally far more observant of their tradition's moral code than members of other religions are of their own codes, which it is pertinent to remark because (again according to the moderates) the ethics of Islam reject the kind of atrocities committed in its name on 11 September 2001 in New York and Washington, and later in Madrid, London, and elsewhere. Moreover, defenders of Islam point to its being a culture of artistic, musical and philosophical richness, which should not be judged by the lunatic severities of extremists such as the Taliban and Al-Qaeda, whose repressive understanding of their religion empties it of its humanity, and returns those who live under their power to medieval darkness.

What the moderate voices say about Islam is welcome and promising. But alas the fact remains that Islam is a fertile breeding ground for extremism because it also lends itself to hard-line interpretations and fundamentalist commitment. Moreover zealot movements in Islam worldwide are funded and encouraged by the wealth enjoyed by some Muslim majority states, not least Saudi Arabia, as a result of their oil and the rest of the world's thirst for oil. The bookshops in mosques in Britain carry Saudi-funded Wahhabi literature denigrating Western culture and extolling purist forms of Islam, adding to the destabilisation of relations between Muslim communities in the West and their host nations. The paradox is stark: as we have seen, Muslim immigration to Europe and North America is prompted by the liberalism, the wealth, the opportunities in health, education and economic life, that the West's way of life makes possible – and then the imams and the Wahhabi books attack the things that the immigrants went to the West for, disaffecting the second and third generations of the immigrant families, already torn between their families' traditions and the inducements of the free societies around them.

These remarks only touch upon the complexities. However they are best analysed, it remains the case that the world is prey to some extremely dangerous, murderous and conscienceless people. One of the reasons why, early in the post-9/11 phase of the terrorist threat (we forget that it existed long before), Osama bin Laden was singled out as a particular target is that he served a propaganda need: a need to personalise and focus the response in order to marshal Western voters behind the effort to drain the swamp – at that point correctly identified as Afghanistan – in which this dangerous spawn swam. Western domestic constituencies had to be encouraged to accept the necessity of military action, and those charged with this task needed a focus; at the tabloid level, explaining what is happening and why difficult things must be done is made greatly easier by personalising and particularising matters.

Nevertheless there were very good reasons for placing bin Laden near the centre of attention. In August 1996 he declared a jihad against the United States. When asked, in the months afterwards, why nothing had yet come of this declaration, he replied, 'the nature of the battle requires good preparation'. Two years later a US embassy in East Africa was bombed with great loss of life, and then a US navy vessel, the destroyer USS *Cole*, was attacked in a Yemen port. The 1998 attacks were significant, because in that year bin Laden widened his jihad decree against the US by saying that its people and interests were to be attacked anywhere in the world.

What explains bin Laden's hostility to the US is his anger on finding, on his return in 1991 from fighting with the CIA-backed Afghan mujahedin against the Soviet Union, that US forces were based in his home country of Saudi Arabia. The forces were there at the invitation of the Saudi government following the 1991 Gulf War, but bin Laden saw them as 'crusaders' who by their presence blasphemed the land which contains the two holiest places of Islam, Mecca and Medina – the reason for this interpretation being that Mohammed had decreed that there should never be two religions in Arabia. Moreover, the Saudi economy suffered in the years after the Gulf War, and bin Laden blamed this on the Saudi government's financial contribution to having US forces based in the country.

In his 1998 decree bin Laden accused America of having declared war on Islam. He accordingly stated his aim to be the expulsion of the 'Judaeo-Christian enemy' from Islam's holy lands. 'The United States is occupying the lands of Islam in the holiest of its territories, Arabia, plundering its riches, overwhelming its rulers, humiliating its peoples, and using it as a base to launch attacks on neighbouring Islamic peoples,' he said.

Osama bin Laden regards the presence of 'Judaeo-Christians' in Saudi Arabia and the hardships experienced by Iraq following the Gulf War as acts of terrorism in themselves, thus retorting on the US the accusation made against himself. And at this point the rhetoric of anger and hatred begins to show. 'Americans plunder our wealth and our resources and our oil,' he said in his 1998 statement. 'Our religion is under attack. They kill and murder our brothers. They compromise our honour and our dignity and dare we utter a single word of protest against the injustice, they call us terrorists.'

An oddity of the situation is that bin Laden, a multi-millionaire Saudi layman, is not in a position to decree jihads against anyone. The promulgation of any fatwah (religious decree) is the province of conclaves of clerics, such as the one called in Afghanistan to pronounce on the demand for bin Laden's extradition.

This same conclave called for a jihad in the event of attacks on Afghanistan. One of the most telling moments occurred when the BBC's John Simpson, broadcasting from the inhospitable border between Pakistan and Afghanistan, optimistically remarked that the Taliban were so unpopular, and their tenure on power so fragile, that their grip on Afghanistan was unlikely to survive a major intervention by Western forces. They were (and remain) more popular in Pakistan than within their own borders, chiefly among hot-headed and resentful Pakistani young men who probably have no conception of what life would really be like under theocratic absolutism, especially of the kind premised on fantastically conservative and rigid interpretations of Islamic law; but who believe it would somehow be in their interests, and anyway a means of impugning America and the West generally.

But bin Laden was not the only likely target in this conflict. Intelligence audits of information from victims who telephoned from the doomed aircraft on 11 September suggested that at least some of the hijackers had Hezbollah connections, and one of them was known to have had contacts with Iraqi representatives in Germany just months before the attacks occurred.

One way the net has to widen is for everyone in the anti-terrorist coalition to make some reappraisals. For one example, they have to see that the IRA was the Al-Qaeda of the Irish and British backyard. If pictures of IRA bombings at Canary Wharf and elsewhere were now shown to Americans who gave money to Noraid and other organisations supporting the IRA, what would their response be? True, there is the complicating fact that some acts committed in the course of resistance struggles are indistinguishable from acts of terrorism: the remark 'one man's terrorist is another man's freedom fighter' poses a challenge to be clear about what deserves the name and what does not. South Africa's Nelson Mandela was removed from the US list of international terrorists shortly before his ninetieth birthday, as one of the last acts of George W. Bush's presidency; this is a mark of the problem some feel in drawing a distinction. To me the difficulty does not always seem great: the struggle against apartheid was not terrorism, the 9/11 atrocities were; more difficult cases can be tested about why we make these judgments.

But there is one further urgent matter, and perhaps in the end it is the most important thought of all. As always with such thoughts, it is vastly easier to state than to put into effect. It is that terrorism in part happens because people who perceive themselves as ignored, contemned, slighted, and unjustly treated, feel that they have no other effective recourse. Part of the misnamed 'War on Terror' has to involve making the world a fairer place, where everyone gets a hearing, and where injustices have a genuine chance of being remedied. Without this, peace is unlikely. 'Getting a hearing' does not mean that what those constituencies want they are invariably going to get. Islamists want all the rest of us to convert to Islam and to subject ourselves to a revived Caliphate and Shari'a law. That is decidedly not going to happen. Getting a hearing on condition of giving others a hearing, compromising, accepting that some of one's desiderata are not going to happen, or not yet, are all marks of grown-up citizenship of the world. Islam is a religion that has a too-ready tendency to infantilise its votaries – the more eager they are, the more unreflective and doctrinaire the pieties substituting for their rationality and maturity, as one sees in the childishly angry demonstrations, inflamed by demagogues, against Danish cartoonists, Salman Rushdie, and the like. (Muslim extremists are not alone in this: Christians, Hindus and Sikhs are perfectly capable of it too.) This is the difficulty of applying the suggested remedy – of inclusion and social justice – which requires maturity of outlook. But it is, short of responding exactly in kind to the terrorists (but vastly more in degree, given the vastly superior and infinitely more destructive arsenals at the West's disposal), the only hope.

Obviously, the bin Ladens and hot-heads are beyond approach on lines of greater social justice and opportunity. But the constituencies whose complicity, even if it is a complicity of silent inaction, allows the terrorists to exist and enact their shocking deeds of mass murder, are fertile ground for such an approach or family of approaches – 'family' because, clearly, different circumstances require suitably tailored initiatives. This is a task for governments and NGOs working in concert to apply well-researched strategies for the medium and long term. The contribution that private citizens can make is to encourage and support the effort, uncertain and drawn-out though it will be.

These thoughts are prompted by the circumstances that Western governments invoke to justify the erosion of civil liberties they cause by their security measures and legislative initiatives. The 'War on Terror' is their prompt and their excuse; I return now to the harm they are thus doing to the values and social fabric of Western democracies.

12

Surveillance and Identity

Western democracies have launched themselves on an unprecedented orgy of surveillance of their entire populations in order to catch or pre-empt the few who do (or might) pose some kind of risk to them through crime or terror.

It is by now a familiar fact that there are more CCTV cameras keeping watch in Britain than in any other country in the world, even in the worst police states. In one way this could be thought unexceptionable, because it can be argued that cameras take the place of policemen on the beat, and far more effectively, thus ensuring public safety and providing a useful adjunct both to the prevention of crime and its punishment.

But it is also a fact that there are a number of ways in which CCTV footage can be misused, or lead to serious error. None are hard to imagine. In the capital of the free world, the USA, individuals were for decades tracked and monitored, and their communications eavesdropped upon, not because they were known terrorists or criminals, but because of their political views and trades union affiliations: this happened from the late 1940s through the McCarthy, civil rights and Vietnam eras until it eventually sparked a constitutional debate in the 1970s. The difference between the US and the former Soviet Union in this respect, vanishingly small while the police snooped on political 'undesirables', was that public outcry and political activism in the former brought a (temporary – until the advent of George W. Bush) halt to sneaking and prying by the state on its citizens.

Consider, then, the fact that some police forces in the UK have seriously considered adding microphones to CCTV cameras in our streets so that they can not only watch what people are doing, but also overhear what they are saying. This is a quantum step from surveillance of the public domain shared by the community to monitoring of the utterances and thereby thoughts and opinions of individuals.

Extraordinarily, it seems that the difference between the public presence of people in shared space and the privacy of their utterances and thoughts was not even considered. The parallel to eavesdropping on people's conversations is putting CCTV cameras inside their houses. At least most people would object very strongly to the latter, even if in half a dozen houses round the realm some crazed fanatics were making bombs in their living rooms.

The claims of security are too readily allowed to override those of civil liberty. As James Madison said, 'The means of defence against foreign danger historically have become the instruments of tyranny at home.' That is why, even in times of danger, one of the truest of commonplaces is that the price of liberty is eternal vigilance. Compare today's situation to the one described by E. M. Forster in his speech (entitled 'Liberty in England') at the *Congrès international des écrivains* in Paris in 1935, when the world was sliding into the abyss of war. He acknowledged the threat posed by the fascist dictators, and then warned of a different, home-grown threat that was in effect the shadow-image of the external threat: 'we are menaced [internally] by what I might call 'Fabio-Fascism,' by the dictator-spirit working quietly away behind the façade of constitutional forms, passing a little law (like the Sedition Act) here, endorsing a departmental tyranny there, emphasising the national need for secrecy elsewhere, and whispering and cooing the so-called "news" every evening over the wireless, until opposition is tamed and gulled. Fabio-Fascism is what I am afraid of, for it is the traditional method by which liberty has been attacked in England. It was the method of King Charles I – a gentleman if ever there was one – the method of our enlightened authoritarian gentlemen today. This Fabio-Fascism is our old enemy, the tyrant ...' and then Forster quoted Kipling:

> He shall mark our goings, question whence we came,
> Set his guards about us, as in Freedom's name.
> He shall peep and mutter, and the night shall bring
> Watchers 'neath our window, lest we mock the King.

Surveillance, identity cards, the reading of emails and the taping of phone calls, eavesdropping on the public as it goes about its daily business, all constitute 'watchers 'neath our window' indeed, and all 'in Freedom's name.' As Forster remarked, 'How well Kipling put it!', anticipating as he did the Orwellian logic of protecting our liberties by taking them away.

One of the instruments proposed as a means of surveillance – a means of keeping track of everyone in order to flush out the few bad people among them – is the use of biometric identity cards, which are in effect barcodes for citizens, an instrument of unique identification easily and readily monitored by any security or government agency with an interest in doing so.

Are ID cards either philosophically or pragmatically justifiable? Emphatically, No. A requirement for every citizen to carry a device that enables the authorities, on demand, to access immediate and conclusive information about them, dramatically changes the relationship of individuals to the state, from being private citizens to being numbered conscripts.

Any individual thus tagged and numbered is a trackable, controllable unit, exposed to continual monitoring if any of the authorities empowered to carry it out choose to do so. In Britain at the beginning of the Second World War identity cards were issued because of the emergency situation, and abolished after the war. At first the ID information was registered with two ministries, the Home Office and the Ministry of Defence. By the end of the war it was accessible to sixty-two government ministries and agencies. This is a classic example of 'mission creep', to which all laws and security instruments are subject.

For more contemporary instances: the British activist Peter Tatchell demonstrated outside the wedding of Prince Charles, heir to the British throne, to Mrs Camilla Parker

Bowles. He did so by holding up a placard saying, 'The Prince of Wales can marry twice, but a gay person cannot marry once.' This was before the introduction of 'civil partnership' arrangements for gay couples. He was arrested and detained under new terrorism laws passed not long beforehand by the United Kingdom Parliament. Under these same laws the Conservative MP Damian Green was detained by police, and his parliamentary office searched, in connection with a leak of information from the Home Office.

Thus history teaches that once an instrument of control lies in the hands of authorities, they will use it and indeed extend its use to unpredicted areas: from 'protecting against terrorism' (if only this were possible in all cases) to catching tax avoiders, to finding defaulting child-support payers to collecting parking fines, to watching members of the Socialist Workers' Party to snooping on individuals against whom rumours and gossip have turned attention: and so endlessly on. Who can guarantee that a government twenty, forty, sixty years hence will be as benign as the one, today, that wishes to tag us all for the greater ease of policing us? In the absence of a guarantee, why create now a giant computerised 'National Identity Register' (what George Orwell would make of this is not hard to guess) ready for the hands of a possibly less benign future?

Among the main proponents of an identity surveillance system are the biometric data companies who stand to gain billions in start-up and recurrent revenue. At time of writing they already say that all the DNA and finger-print details that will link one to the computer where address, bank, medical, employment records, and more, are collated, can be stored on a chip the size of the following full-stop. This can be implanted in one's earlobe, ostensibly to protect against loss or theft, and can be read by a device similar to a supermarket bar-code reader. I once asked politician and government minister Mr David Milliband what the difference is between this and a number branded on one's arm. His furious response was not an answer, but proof that I had cut close to a nerve.

Making 'identity recognition' a precious commodity will create a huge new criminal industry dedicated to stealing, forging and manipulating identity cards or devices. It is said that a well-known motor vehicle manufacturer devised a thumbprint security system for their cars, claiming that this was a far safer system than any involving the use of keys; and that a prototype was stolen by thieves who simply cut the thumb off the car's owner in order to drive his car away. If we have little biometric data identity chips implanted in our earlobes, are we destined to become a nation of Van Goghs so that thieves can access our bank accounts and votes?

No informed individual or agency, other than the government and the biometric data companies anticipating large revenues, wants the ID scheme. At a meeting I attended in the Palace of Westminster in early 2007 (and subsequently reported in detail in a special issue of the magazine *New Statesman*) experts ranging from an assistant commissioner of the Metropolitan Police to academics to electronic engineers discussed the ID card scheme with a government minister, and unanimously condemned it as unworkable, over-costly, and an invasion of liberties.

13

Identity for Sale

Every time a member of the government defends the introduction of ID cards, a new ground is offered to justify them. Their first proponent, Home Secretary David Blunkett, first said they were needed to counter terrorism, and then said they were needed to catch illegal immigrants. He attempted to change their name from 'identity cards' to 'entitlement cards', saying that they would be necessary to gain access to health and welfare services. And they were also claimed to be necessary in the fight against crime, including identity theft itself.

One effort, by no less a personage than Tony Blair when Prime Minister, is very revealing. In the pubic setting of a news conference he said that the question of identity cards (along with other matters such as anti-social behaviour orders, CCTV cameras and a DNA database) are not about civil liberties but about 'modernity', meaning that in these modern times we must use new technology to tackle what he calls 'new' types of crime.

There is almost too much to say about this remark and the mindset it reveals. For those who wish to argue from 'we have the technology' to 'let's use it therefore' as Mr Blair there did, in respect of cloning, embryo research, nuclear weapons, and so indefinitely on, this is a highly useful piece of illogicality. It surely does not need saying, in response, that for each and every individual possibility offered by technology, a separate case has to be made for its acceptability. In my view the answers would come out: cloning and embryo research, Yes; nuclear weapons, No; mass surveillance and invasion of privacy of the national population, No.

But what lies behind Mr Blair's slip of the mind is the following. The three constituencies who stand to gain most from the introduction of identity cards are (1) the security services, because identity cards are, as we have seen, tracking devices, making it easy for the entire population to be policed. A reader device in a police car will bring up any individual's data on the 'National Identity Register', a fact that prompts one to wonder how long before arbitrary identity checks become a norm of life on British streets; (2) criminals, for whom the theft and forging of identity devices will quickly become a major industry; and (3) the biometric data companies who stand to make many billions of pounds of income from setting up the system, issuing the first tens of millions of cards, replacing the further millions lost or stolen every year, changing information on them every time someone moves or marries or has some other significant change in life, and selling brand new cards every year to newly come-of-age children and immigrants – and this, richly and to massive profit, in perpetuity.

Now Mr Blair's 'modernity' point – we have the technology, so let us use it – gives the game away as regards this last. Biometric data companies push as hard as they can to open the floodgates of this revenue stream into their bank accounts – revenue from the sale of our personal identities and our civil liberties. Asking *cui bono?* (who benefits?) has its uses here.

To substantiate the claim that the biometric data companies are one of the main impetuses behind the ID card scheme, the following tale offers a relevant parallel. A few years ago I sat on an independent commission, funded by the Rowntree Trust, into the question of drug testing in the workplace. Pharmaceutical companies had devised a small kit for testing individuals for drug use, and seeking a market for them they went to businesses and asked, 'What if one of your employees is under the influence of drugs, and does something that makes you liable to being sued by a customer? Here is a handy kit you can use to test your employees' recreational habits.'

Of course, we do not want our airline pilots and taxi drivers to be drugged or hung-over at work. But for the vast majority of employees, what they ingested or inhaled at the weekend is no one's business but their own – unless the law in some way becomes involved. The pharmaceutical companies were marketing a privacy-invading technology for profit; our commission aimed to forestall the usual reaction of government ('dog bites child, shoot all the dogs') to the challenges that use of the kits might offer. The problem is clear to see: given the prospect of substantial income, makers of new technologies will do everything they can to sell them, questions of civil liberties taking a back seat. Biometric data companies are doing exactly the same in the identity card matter. But commercial imperatives and innovations cannot be allowed to take the public debate hostage.

Mr Blair reprised the spurious argument that we all already have so many cards – credit cards, store cards, loyalty cards, a passport, a driving licence – that one more will not hurt, and indeed will be a convenience. The great difference is that we have each of these other cards voluntarily; we choose to enter into an individual relationship with a retail store or the Automobile Association, or to drive or to travel. Lacking some of these cards would be an inconvenience, certainly, but there is a world of difference between a voluntary arrangement with a specific organisation for a specific purpose, and being obliged by law to have your personal information stored on a central government computer and linked to an identity card that the authorities are empowered to inspect on demand.

The fact that Blair, a lawyer by training, was not concerned about the question of principle here is deeply troubling. It took centuries for the British people to achieve the civil liberties we have. Some of those liberties have been temporarily suspended during times of war. But now, 'because the technology is there' and despite the fact that the present level of threat is tiny in comparison to the threat of invasion in 1941, the government proposes to introduce *permanent* reductions in our civil liberties. Either our governments do not see this, or do not care because they prioritise other considerations; but either way the situation does them no credit.

Defenders of identity card schemes say (and this is their standard line) that the first priority of government is to protect the populace against crime and terrorism. This is false. The first priority of government is to protect our liberties. That does not mean that protecting security is not also a high priority; but it is emphatically not the highest. Liberties worth having carry a risk; a mature society should accept the risk. To repeat, as one endlessly must, what Benjamin Franklin said, 'Those who would sacrifice liberty for security deserve neither.'

One of the civil liberties most violated by an ID card scheme and all the other means of surveillance is of course privacy. Every human rights convention accords individuals the right of privacy; every intrusion of surveillance violates that right. I turn attention to it next.

14

Privacy

No human rights convention is complete without an article that defends privacy, for the excellent reason that privacy is an indispensable adjunct of the minimum that individuals require for a chance to build good lives. One aspect of its importance is that it gives people a measure of control over the front they offer others, and the amount of information that others have about them, concerning matters that are personal, intimate, eccentric or constitutive of the individual's inner life.

Moreover, most of the plans and projects that matter to people are too fragile in their early phases to bear much examination from others, and need therefore to be protected from view until they are sufficiently matured. Even more so are relationships in need of a private space for their nourishment and development, away from the gaze of others, including even other family members.

But the foremost reason for privacy is that it is crucial for personal autonomy and psychological well-being. Even lovers require a degree of privacy from each other, for to lack a reserve of selfhood is almost the same as not having a self at all.

At the same time we are all curious about others' lives and doings. A central reason for this is that insights into others' experience is an important adjunct to reflection on our own experience, and they help us to understand and manage our own lives better. Malicious gossip and harmful rumours aside, the sharing of information about human experience is an essential component of being part of human experience, and we could not do without it. How else could we satisfy ourselves so well about whether we are normal, or succeeding, or coping, or in need of reorganising ourselves – and so usefully on.

It follows that there is no dishonesty in wishing to peep (figuratively speaking) through others' windows, even though there are large margins of information which we have no right to acquire about others. The desire to pry, and the illegitimacy of prying, are both facts we have to accept: we have to live with the disappointment as this applies to others, and relief as it applies to ourselves. The two are mutually informative, and jointly explain why a right to privacy is such a fundamental right. We try to discover as much as we can about others, and to reveal as little of ourselves to others as possible, except when we wish to include others in the sphere of our privacy, and to get intimately into theirs.

A larger question concerns interference by government in individual privacy for purposes of combating crime and terrorism. It can be argued that one of the prices to be paid for security is the compromise of privacy in relevant respects – principally the interception of communications. This has to be done on warrant, with review and proper controls, and always for a strictly defined purpose and with a time limit. Anything else is the stuff of Orwell's *1984*. The signal point is the line between this and what people do in their private lives and their own homes. If consenting adults get up to activities that more timid souls might construe as involving harm to themselves, the state – this is Mill's inviolable and irrefutable principle – has no business knowing about it, let alone interfering with it.

There are always regions of uncertainty in the business of managing society: they have to be considered strictly on their merits, but always under control of the principle that when there is any doubt in the case, let privacy trump curiosity and the activities of the police.

Any discussion of matters of principle benefits from looking at individual cases. Since the erosion of British civil liberties began under the stewardship of Mr Tony Blair when he was Prime Minister, it is salutary to recall his own feelings and – contrasting – actions relating to the matter of privacy.

If there was one respect in which Mr Blair's concerns reflected those of contemporary British society, it was in his ambivalence over the question of privacy. He wished his youngest child's christening to be private, and was vexed by press intrusion into it. But after threatening in revenge to cancel the traditional photo call of his family on its summer holiday, he recanted. According to Lord Wakeham, then chairman of the Press Complaints Commission, his decision to let the paparazzi get their holiday snaps struck the best balance between 'legitimate privacy and legitimate public interest'.

It is mystifying how photographs of a prime minister's family on holiday serve any public interest, but not in the least mystifying why public figures should wish to ration the press's access to their family lives, especially for their children's sake. At the same time, all public figures live and die by publicity, needing it as fuel, as platform, as justification, as the source of popularity when things go well, and as an instrument for influencing public opinion. That means temporising with their own and their families' privacy in order to keep the dangerous relationship with the media alive. After all, images of a prime minister as family man obviously go down well with electors, and for that reason Mr Blair was never likely to keep the cameras from his family for long.

The Blairs' privacy ambivalences came at an interesting time. They coincided with Mr Blair's government's action of equipping the police and secret services with new surveillance powers over the populace's email and internet activities, increasing the means for official invasion of privacy. At the very same time, the European Court of Human Rights at Strasbourg had just found against the United Kingdom in the case of a gay man prosecuted for what he and friends did in his home. The Strasbourg decision proved crucial in persuading the Home Office, then reviewing indecency laws, to abandon mooted provisions criminalising private sexual activity. Three cheers for Europe.

Debate over these matters reflects the divided relationship contemporary society has with privacy. It is accordingly of value to go over the ground as to the subtle but important difference between individual curiosity and official invasions of privacy. As we have seen, on the one hand most of us are deeply interested in other people and what they get up to, a fact which explains what at first seems widely disparate phenomena. In large numbers people consume, with relish, tabloid newspaper gossip and revelations about 'celebrities', morning television chat shows where ordinary folk make extraordinary confessions, soap operas where we can all be invisible spies observing fictionalised versions of other lives, the egregious Big Brother series where viewers witness 'real lives' (or more accurately the boredom and occasional folly of people cooped together in an artificial setting) – and of course the more traditional staples of film, drama, biographies and novels. All these sources of data about other people answer an important need: our voyeuristic impulse to research human experience continually, as a way of informing ourselves about life's meanings and possibilities.

Such voyeurism of this necessary and universal kind cannot be content with observing the outward manifestations of others' lives. It needs to get as much into their privacies as possible, eager to uncover what they really do and think. We are hungry for the low-down, the gritty truth, the unvarnished details. A relish for snooping is, according to everyday morality, a bad thing; but it is a necessary thing, and an unstoppable one.

But all of this is individual curiosity, not government spying; and we all know that it can go too far – that it has its limits.

At the same time, and in direct contradiction to this individual form of voyeurism, we all need privacy as much as we need sustenance. Few of us can function without a private life. In the circle of family or chosen friends we can express ourselves naturally, and behave without artifice – in short, we can relax. A hidden microphone, or a telephoto lens that captures our intimate contacts, is a violation of what is central to personal well-being. From prime ministers to other celebrities to ordinary citizens, having a moat of privacy around them is not a luxury but a necessity, a constitutive aspect of well-being, and a right that neither the press nor the security services should be allowed to breach without an absolutely water-tight justification.

15

Democracy

One of the most important ideas in discussion of the broader setting of civil liberties, and which all countries that claim to have and to value civil liberties also value, is democracy.

When Chinese students occupied Tiananmen Square in the fateful summer of 1989, they raised in their midst a statue they called 'the Goddess of Democracy'. In 1979 their older siblings, destined to a less bloody suppression by China's authorities, turned a length of Peking brick into 'Democracy Wall', where freedom of expression briefly flourished in the form of fly-posters. In both cases the name and spirit of democracy were summoned to oppose the rule of the Communist Party of China.

China still waits for democracy, but the sacrifice of Tiananmen Square did much to make possible the revolutions in Eastern Europe later in 1989. The crowds there likewise invoked democracy, and people in the West applauded. 'Democracy' is a feel-good word; it is what the West officially stands for and defends. Who would now dream of saying – at least, aloud – that oligarchy or plutocracy or dictatorship is preferable? One might criticise democracy, but only to end by describing it as the best of an imperfect set of alternatives.

It has not always been so. The history of anti-democratic sentiment in Western civilisation from classical Athens to the present is a chastening tale with many morals, whose chief point is that until recently democracy was vilified as the despotism of poor, ignorant, unthinking majorities over better-off and better-educated minorities. Since most of those able to record their opinions belonged to the latter class, history resounds with their condemnation of any political arrangement that allowed the Great Unwashed a say in affairs of state.

Athens in the fifth and fourth centuries BCE was not a democracy in anything like the true sense of the world (women, slaves and aliens had no say, and men only reached adulthood at thirty), though it styled itself one, meaning that all enfranchised adult males were equal citizens with an equal say in the running of the state. But at its height under Pericles the Athenian democracy produced art, architecture, drama and philosophy of such power and excellence that they continue to shape Western civilisation.

Yet even then the idea of democracy had its opponents. The aristocratic Plato attacked it for putting management of the state into the hands of ignoramuses unable to distinguish right from wrong. He blamed it for making the citizenry 'idle, cowardly, loquacious and greedy' and for devouring those – Pericles, Miltiades, Themistocles – who had promoted it in the first place.

With the leading philosophers of Athens against it, democracy had little chance among later thinkers.

Renaissance writers were convinced it meant constant tumult. Enlightenment moralists saw it as a threat to virtue. America's founding fathers believed it led to the equalisation of property. And when the grudging shift to something approaching democracy happened in Britain during the century between 1830 and 1930, its opponents claimed they were being sold to the rabble. For them, the image of democracy was the Paris mob of the early 1790s.

What has lately made democracy not just respectable but something to die for? One answer is: the work of nineteenth-century historians, who rescued Athenian democracy from the opprobrium of earlier historians. This thesis is more plausible than it seems, for intellectual sentiment diffuses itself like dew in the night, and democratic ideas are not the only ones to achieve resurrection because later thinkers reversed the judgements of their predecessors. In associating democratic ideals with the glories of Periclean Athens, the theory of democracy was at last made respectable.

But for how long? Some critics take a view of more than merely theoretical importance: that whereas conservative theory and practice in America has resulted in devolution of political authority, British conservatism has effected a rapid centralisation of power, breaking with its own traditions by weakening or abolishing intermediary institutions like local government.

The British swing to authoritarianism is arguably the alarmed reaction, once voiced by Michael Oakshott and others mainly on the political right, to perceived national decline. British political institutions have always been carefully and unobtrusively arranged to dissipate the effects of democracy, a fact as welcomed by Labour politicians when in office as by Conservative politicians at all times. As national and international affairs grow more difficult to manage, and the future less certain with each new crisis, whether induced by terrorism or financial difficulties in world markets and banking systems, secret and managed hostility to democratic ideas in Western societies might become less secret and more managed.

There is some force in the dismaying thought that the world's so-far relatively brief experiment in democracy is proving hard for ordinary folk to admire, or even bear. This is not least because politicians in democracies have learned how to nullify or control the power of the voting public by various kinds of manipulation, and also because people feel a certain weariness generated by the gap between politician's promises and the hard realities – which are that things take a lot of turning around, inertia is deep in the system, vested interests are organised, well funded and influential in ways that disempower voters who are insufficiently organised and have their say only periodically. The lobbyists are in the corridors of power every day, cheque books in hand – and always therefore better poised to win.

One of the more interesting commentators on democracy and its fate is the thinker Hannah Arendt. Her chief importance rests on her writings about the nature and effects of totalitarianism. She famously coined the expression 'the banality of evil' after observing the trial of Adolf Eichmann in Jerusalem in the early 1960s. Her key idea is that totalitarian regimes function by organising the internally fragmented mass of individuals around a simplistic ideology, using such 'elements of shame' as racism and imperialism so that even the vilest deeds can be performed with bureaucratic blandness and without troubling the good conscience of ordinary people.

As regards democracy, Arendt warned against the risk of the mass's increasing disengagement from political activity, a risk she saw as implicit in contemporary society's materialistic obsessions. This mattered urgently to her, for whom political engagement is one of the most important aspects of life, because it concerns the character of human social existence. In her view the risk of political disengagement is that people become morally superficial, and as a result vulnerable to exploitation by demagogues.

Arendt was struck by Adolf Eichmann's inability to think for himself. She saw that he lacked imagination, was narrow and dim, and had 'the horrible gift of consoling himself with clichés'. He refused to read Nabokov's *Lolita* when offered it in prison, on the grounds that it was 'unwholesome'. This fact shocked observers, who could not comprehend, and still less stomach, his lack of any sense of moral measure. He had thought, he told the court, that he was being a good state servant by following orders, by doing what he was told. The clash between the 'goodness' of loyalty and the evil of what it effected was the point of most intense interest for Arendt. From the insight it afforded sprang her remark that evil can be banal, for it can be carried out with an easy conscience by people who are neither monsters or madmen.

What Arendt did not see is that although the middle-men of evil are often as Eichmann was – and indeed, all the more to be feared for their lack either of insight or courage – the true fountain of evil in regimes like that of the Nazis is anything but banal. Rather, it is passionate and violent, highly theorised, a creed and a commitment, put into massive and tragic effect by people who know what they are doing and believe in it. It is to them and not only to their servants that one has to look for an understanding of inhumanity and the disasters it brings.

So the passionate and the committed are a greater danger to democracy than the banal and managerial, and the former can mobilise the latter to undermine the democracy they know how to manage and manipulate. Both represent a threat to the fragile promise that the least bad of all systems of governance represents; it is as well to remember that the enemies of all good or least bad things exist within as well as without.

The clumsy electoral mechanism operative in the United Kingdom allows the largest minority of those qualified to vote – which includes the citizens of many foreign states, including Eire – to put what is in effect an oligarchy into power for four or five years (the late Quintin Hogg, Lord Hailsham, called the House of Commons 'an elected tyranny'). The electoral system does this without providing a means of controlling the oligarchy's behaviour in the interval between elections, if its crazy electoral arithmetic gives one party an absolute majority in the House of Commons. This matters because the Commons has, if it wishes to use it, an almost absolute discretion of power; only the delaying powers of judicial review and the House of Lords, and the recent advent of the

Human Rights Act, has placed tentative constraints on it, all of which can easily be shrugged off by means of further Commons legislation or repeal.

The once-vaunted liberties of the British subject are thus wholly at the sufferance of the party of the largest minority – everything from the freedom of the press to the freedom of individual movement. One thing and one only rescues this perilous edifice from absolutely corrupting those thus in power: the British tradition of suffering the press to be free, even (to a reasonable extent) in wartime. For this means that the public are offered a competition of interpretations of what the government of the day is doing, which now and then inflames public sentiment sufficiently to chasten that government – its eye on the next election and the arithmetic of minorities – into ecstasies of spin, and if that does not work, at last into adjusting its tiller.

Let us return, for its lessons, to the history of the idea of democracy. In the Athens of Cleisthenes and Pericles democracy meant, as noted, a democracy of the adult male minority of the population. But the ideal of equal status for the enfranchised, and the practical effect of their involvement in the government of the state, set the tone: this first coming of democracy carried significant seeds. Plato hated it, and for the next two millennia and more, for the reasons explained above, so did everyone else except for levellers, dreamers, the poor and the oppressed.

The second coming of democracy occurred in the eighteenth century, transfigured by the alchemy of time and circumstance into the doctrines of the American and French revolutions. This story would be best told by picking exactly the right topics to dwell upon in each case: for the story of American democracy, James Madison's reinterpretation of the idea of a democracy into the idea of a republic, whose key is representation; and in the French case, the significance of Babeuf's Conspiracy during Thermidor, and what it meant for the democratic idea in that turbulent moment of its rebirth.

But here we are in the twenty-first century still asking, 'Why Democracy?' The world of the contemporary 'democracies' is a disenchanted and demoralised one, which one perceptive commentator characterises as 'all too well adjusted to lives organised around the struggle to maximise personal income'. It has none of the glamour of the age of Pericles. Such admiration as individual politicians might sometimes command during their tenure of office vanishes rapidly away under the sceptical, faithless and cynical scrutiny of press and public. 'Over the two centuries in which [democracy] has come to triumph,' John Dunn wrote in *Setting the People Free* (Atlantic, 2005), 'some have seen it simply as an impostor, bearer of a name which it has stolen, and instrument for the rule of the people by something unmistakably different.'

Is there an answer to current disenchantment with democracy, and the perception of its failure? Is talk of democracy nothing more than a convenience for a system which benefits a particular economic order, and a rationalisation of its legitimacy?

It is not good enough merely to hope that this latter is not the case. We have to do more: we have to stand up and change it. That almost certainly means thinking about a new

16

We the People

The story of how the Constitution of the United States of America was created is a stirring one, for it represents perhaps the greatest achievement of the eighteenth-century Enlightenment. It was much more radical an event even than the French Revolution, which began in 1789 not as an effort to institute a republic but to fashion a constitutional monarchy like England's. In the revolted British colonies of North America the aim was bolder: it was to fashion a democratic republic from scratch, the closest available model for which was pre-imperial Rome. Despite their human failings and partisan foibles, the men who devised the US Constitution were as great as the most principled of ancient Rome's senators – Cicero and Cato spring to mind – and their endeavour was no less significant than anything the Romans did. Perhaps, indeed, it was more so.

There were two main reasons why the Americans needed to devise a Constitution. One was that the colonies had been independent of one another, though not of the British crown, until some form of federation or confederation was proposed as the alternative to the trans-Atlantic dependence; so a way of agreeing the relationship was necessary. The second was that the colonists (both the first colonists and the waves of immigration since) had gone to America to be as independent as possible of the constraints, even tyrannies, of forced religious orthodoxies and monarchical rule in Europe. When George III behaved towards his North American possessions as Louis XIV had earlier behaved in France, the independent-minded colonists objected; the rest is history.

American opponents of the idea of a federal United States argued instead for a looser confederation which would leave political authority in the states themselves. They argued that it is a mistake to think in terms of a single overriding public interest shared by all citizens of a state; different people have different interests, and wish to have those interests represented and indeed acted upon; they have a right to this, and to organise themselves into parties in order to ensure that their interests have the best chance of being promoted. This pluralistic view denies that the ideas of 'the many' or 'the majority' have political reality; there is instead a great number of diverse individuals and groups, and whatever political structures are built must reflect this fact.

The Federalists, by contrast, argued that there is such a thing as 'the public good', and that it is possible to identify 'the *real* welfare of the great body of the people' (as Madison put it). In the debate over the proposed Constitution, which lasted from the autumn of 1787 until it was at last ratified in 1789, three of those closely associated with drafting it – James Madison, Alexander Hamilton and John Jay – wrote in support of it in a series of articles published under the name

'Publius' in a New York newspaper. (Their anti-Federalist opponents used the name 'Cato'.) The *Federalist Papers* together constitute a remarkable document, not only because of the high quality of the writing and argument, but because it is in effect the canon of a novel order, instituting an entirely new republic on the best principles that experience and Enlightenment reflection on them taught. When the *Papers* were collected and published in volume form, Alexander Hamilton (who wrote most of them) provided a general introduction, in which he began by saying, 'It has been frequently remarked that it seems to have been reserved to the people of this country, by their conduct and example, to decide the important question, whether societies of men are really capable or not of establishing good government from reflection and choice, or whether they are forever destined to depend for their political constitutions on accident and force. If there be any truth in the remark, the crisis at which we are arrived may with propriety be regarded as the era in which that decision is to be made; and a wrong election of the part we shall act may, in this view, deserve to be considered as the general misfortune of mankind.'

It comes as a surprise to learn that the authors of the *Papers* were not in favour of a bill of rights to accompany the constitution. When one was adopted it was in part because some of the anti-Federalists' arguments in favour of one had prevailed. In 'Federalist No. 84' Hamilton surveyed the history of bills of rights, describing them as 'in their origin stipulations between kings and their subjects, abridgements of prerogative in favour of privilege, reservations of rights not surrendered to the prince'. For this reason 'they have

no application to constitutions professedly founded upon
the power of the people, and executed by their immediate
representatives and servants'. Only one statement was
required to secure all the rights that a free people anyway
possessed, as shown by the fact that it had instituted its own
government, and it was expressed in the Constitution: 'We
the people of the United States … [to] secure the blessings of
liberty to ourselves and our posterity, do ordain and establish
this Constitution for the United States of America.' What
could be clearer? Moreover, Hamilton said, bills of rights are
not only unnecessary but a positive danger, by suggesting that
they are protections from powers which do not exist – thus,
protecting free speech appears to imply that there is a power
somewhere that limits free speech, but there is in fact no
such power, so no such exemption from it is required. 'Why
for instance, should it be said, that the liberty of the press
shall not be restrained, when no power is given by which
restrictions may be imposed? I will not contend that such a
provision would confer a regulating power; but it is evident
that it would furnish, to men disposed to usurp, a plausible
pretence for claiming that power.'

The argument did not prevail for good reason. Jefferson, in
a letter to Madison, said, 'A Bill of Rights is what the people
are entitled to against every government on earth, general
or particular, and what no just government should refuse or
rest on inference.' Almost all the states already had their own
bills of rights, and there had been a general outcry when it
became apparent that none had been proposed alongside the
Constitution. Hamilton's argument was regarded as especially
sophistical. In the event five of the states voted to ratify the

Constitution only on the proviso that a bill of rights would be subjoined, and almost all the states submitted lists of rights that they wished to see included in such a bill.

The states' bills of rights echoed the words of John Locke, whose writings were a major influence on the Founding Fathers in general. For example, the Virginia Bill of Rights states that people 'have certain inherent rights, of which, when they enter a state of society they cannot by any compact deprive or divest their posterity'. But although the US Bill of Rights encapsulated the fundamental agreement between them all, it emphasised an extra dimension besides that only some of them specified: the right to pursue happiness. That is a very Enlightenment notion.

Madison in his contributions to the *Federalist Papers* saw both the need for the checks and balances, and the danger of partisan politics. The latter he discussed in 'Federalist No. 10', which had the twofold purpose both of advancing suggestions on how to mitigate the effects of factionalism, which he regarded as inevitable, and opposing the anti-Federalists. The aims came together in his saying that the best defence against factionalism is a large republic, not a small one as each individual state would be under the anti-Federalists' preferred alternative. And this is the only way of protecting liberty while allowing for a plurality of interests in the republic, the existence of which is itself a safeguard; because the more such groups there are, the less likely it is that any one of them – any single faction – will be able to dominate the rest.

The anti-Federalist reply, here relying also on Montesquieu's claim that 'It is natural to a republic to have only a small territory, otherwise it cannot long subsist', was that the United States is simply too diverse in its geography, climate, people and existing arrangements to admit of a 'consolidated republican form of government' as George Clinton wrote. The principle of pluralism would be compromised by it, and far from interest groups proving a restraint on the dominance of any faction, they would be the more easily swamped.

There were other questions that the drafters faced but fudged, the most significant being that of slavery. If proof were needed that the drafters were neither infallible nor perfect, this gives it; yet they managed to overcome serious difficulties and differences, in the process producing something original, powerful, and hopeful: the beginnings of something that could be (and at times has been) a great democratic republic.

Constitutional arrangements have to be ajdusted to take account of changing circumstances; the US has done this by means of an accumulation of Amendments. In the case of the UK, the great amendment now required is to have a written constitution, because the unwritten constitution (or, more accurately, *largely* unwritten constitution) that served so well for centuries has now been broken by circumstance, and by incompetence both in regard to practice and principle. But this is a debate for another place and time.

17

Civil Liberties and Human Rights

The concept of 'civil liberties' is virtually synonymous with the concept of 'human rights', though one could argue that there is a small difference in one sense, that the concept of 'human rights' is broader than the concept of 'civil liberties' in that the idea of human rights includes rights to work, fair remuneration, education, health care, and other basics of the possibility of a good life, whereas civil liberties specifically concern those aspects of individual citizenship such as free speech, privacy and individual liberty which are central to it. The distinction is unimportant; the community of the two concepts is the important thing.

For this reason it is well worth reminding ourselves, as a supplement to the discussions above, of an important document in the history of our contemporary world: the Universal Declaration of Human Rights (UDHR), adopted by the United Nations at a meeting in Paris on 10 December 1948.

Writing about revolutionary France's 'Declaration of the Rights of Man', Tom Paine said, 'The first three articles comprehend in general terms the whole of a Declaration of Rights.' That remark applies as much to the UDHR as to the historic document Paine had in mind. In both cases the first three articles are, still to use Paine's words, 'the base of Liberty, as well individual as national; nor can any country be called free whose government does not take its beginning from the principles they contain'.

In the UDHR those principles are that every human individual is born free and equal; that there is no basis for discrimination, on any ground of race, sex, language, opinion and more, to deprive individuals of the rights attributed to them in the Declaration; and that all individuals have the right to life, liberty and security of person.

The first thing a sceptic might say is, Who says? On what grounds are these attributions made? The second thing he might say is, What do these vaporous generalities anyway mean? And the third is, Suppose you can answer the first two questions satisfactorily, where are the big guns to enforce them?

Take for example Article 3. At first appearance it seems to cram too much in: 'life, liberty and security of person' is a portmanteau phrase, its clarity and generality inversely proportional when compared to Article 2 of the European Convention on Human Rights, which is only about a right to life, and slightly more specific about what the 'right to life' means – namely, that no one shall be deprived of life 'intentionally' (except, it questionably goes on to say, under a capital sentence provided by law; curiously, it forgets to license also death through military action by an appointed soldiery).

But there are two resources for clarification of Article 3 and its two predecessors: the Preamble and the other articles of the UDHR itself, together with the immediate background to its drafting. The drafting occurred in the years immediately following 1945; so in saying, as the Preamble's second paragraph does, 'Whereas disregard and contempt for human rights have resulted in barbarous acts which have outraged the conscience of mankind ...' the intention of the first three articles becomes crystal clear. In the light of the Holocaust and other atrocities of war, that intention is to assert, as the default position, a status of inviolability for the human individual, independently of any other fact about him or her. For a central example, it opposes forcing him onto a train, transporting him to a death camp, and murdering him in a gas chamber there. And as a corollary it implies that there has to be a very good reason indeed for the life, the equality, the liberty or the security of individuals to be abrogated, a reason that will override those rights in the light of some more powerful consideration – such as, for example, their forfeiture by a sufficiently serious criminal act justifying deprivation of an individual's liberty.

The effect of the articles is to prise open a space, and then to protect it, in which individuals can exercise choices and capacities to make the best of their other circumstances – although here too the UDHR is ambitious and stipulative, claiming that education and decently remunerated employment are also rights.

Obviously enough the aim of the first three articles is to erect a presumption of rights as a stockade around individuals to shield them from arbitrary attack. It is to guard them against becoming prey to the unscrupulous and the more powerful, against hostile majorities, and against tyrannical government. To the sceptic who asks 'Who says that individuals have these rights?' the argument of experience about the minimum required for a chance of human flourishing, and the recent vivid history of circumstances in which millions were regarded as not having any such rights, is a definitive reply.

The UDHR was devised as an exhortatory document, a statement of aspirations; its Preamble says that it is a proclamation of 'a common standard of achievement for all peoples and all nations', and enjoins UN member states and their citizens to 'strive … to promote respect' for them. So although the emphatic rhetoric of the articles makes them sound formal and legalistic, their force is primarily moral. That does not by one jot make them less important. They express an attitude and a determination, and pave the way for the two great UN Covenants, respectively on civil and political rights and on social and economic rights, that followed them.

Whatever one thinks about the wording of the first three articles, it is hard to gainsay what they aspire to lay down as minimum conditions for a human life worth the name. Nothing less could possibly do.

Article 4 of the UDHR proscribes 'slavery or servitude'; Article 5 states that 'no one shall be subjected to torture or to cruel, inhuman or degrading treatment'. Next to the arbitrary murder of others on the alleged ground that they are inferior to oneself racially, doctrinally, or in some other way, slavery and torture are unquestionably the most abhorrent violations of human rights.

Yet there are few major states in the world, not even those that most loudly proclaim the virtues of liberty and democracy, which are guiltless of subjecting some of their enemies and indeed some of their own citizens to torture or at least inhuman and degrading treatment: not the United States, not the United Kingdom, certainly not the People's Republic of China.

Shall we not torture the man who knows where the dirty nuclear bomb is hidden in the city centre? A utilitarian would not hesitate to water-board him, or push the bamboo splinters up behind his nails. Some make this question a test for how serious one is about individual rights. The drafters had in mind rape of women in conquered populations, the use of prisoners for bayonet practice, the abandonment of starving prisoners to languish in their own excrement. The test case question and the question of civilised behaviour generally – for which the test is surely the same – are part of the same debate. When we think of these things in moments of calm reflection, where principles are best identified and explained, none of these things seems acceptable. But if so, they are still unacceptable when we are worried, frightened, angry, under pressure, and under attack.

As to slavery: according to UN figures, there are more people enslaved today than the total carried to the Americas in three centuries of the Atlantic slave trade: twelve million. Slavery takes many guises and bears many different names now, but it is 'slavery and servitude' nonetheless, characterised by coercion, lack of remuneration, and lack of choice.

One of the standard objections to the UDHR is that it is a Western, Enlightenment invention, and that its claim to universality is spurious. Few things refute this allegation so swiftly as thoughts of torture and slavery. The mammalian nervous system, and what coercion involves, are the conclusive data. For my money these thoughts govern how we should treat all animals generally; so if cows and chickens should not be treated cruelly, still less should any human be so treated. So much for relativism.

Doubts about the UDHR's universality were voiced early, and not at first by people in colonised and developing countries, who welcomed the UDHR with open arms (it was the big powers who were suspicious of it, as threatening to interfere in the exercise of their dominance), but rather by some in the Western world itself. In 1947 the American Anthropological Association voiced concern that ideas of human rights are ethnocentric, and in their submission to Eleanor Roosevelt's committee urged that it take account of the relativity of values to culture, and the point that since an individual 'realizes his personality through his culture, respect for individual differences entails respect for cultural differences'. The trouble with this, as just noted, is that pain and privation are not respecters of culture.

In any case, cultural bias is not always a bad thing. Those cultures that condemn genital mutilation of girls are justified in condemning the cultures that practice it, because they can make a case that members of the latter cultures would be bound to accept in other respects. Thus, if asked if they wish to be protected from harm (say, from having their homes burned and livelihoods destroyed), from pain and mutilation (say, from having a hot poker plunged into their eyes), and from imposed dangers to health (say, from poison being put into their water supplies), they would presumably answer Yes. Then the entirely objective fact that female circumcision and vaginal infibulation are all three of these things, together with a challenge to assumptions about the putative importance of virginity and the claim that male sexual pleasure has an importance that overrides the health and well-being of their wives, ought to settle the matter for any open-minded and normally intelligent person.

Again, so much for relativism. And that is an important point, because Articles 4 and 5 are an explication of Article 3's 'life, liberty and security', and show that it applies without borders.

No fewer than six consecutive articles of the UDHR – 6 to 11 – concern themselves with law. They constitute the single largest grouping in the entire document. Why so many? Giving an answer involves pulling up some deep roots.

For much of the last eight centuries England (specifically England) was regarded as a model for the rest of the world because of the liberties enjoyed by its citizens, offering a sharp contrast to autocratic regimes everywhere from Versailles to Kyoto. In the eighteenth century Voltaire attributed English liberty to the constitution of the people rather than to the constitution of the state; English individualism and independent-mindedness, he implied, were the bulwark of their liberty rather as their navy was the bulwark of their land.

But there was in fact a constitutional provision that underlay the Englishman's vaunted liberty: the provision in Magna Carta – the only one that directly concerned everyone in society irrespective of rank or occupation – that said, 'No freeman is to be taken or imprisoned or destroyed except by the lawful judgment of his peers, or by the law of the land. To no one will we sell, to none will we deny or delay, right or justice.'

Some think that this provision is the origin of *habeas corpus*, which requires anyone who restrains the liberty of another to bring that person to court and there show good reason why he is restrained. If the court is not satisfied with the explanation, it is obliged to order his release. Others say that Magna Carta simply confirms what had long been part of Anglo-Saxon common law.

Either way, the larger idea implicit here is that of 'due process of law' – compare the Fifth Amendment of the US Bill of Rights, which guarantees that 'no person shall be deprived of life, liberty or property without due process of law'. Due process is a safeguard against arbitrary interference with an individual's rights; the idea of rights is practically meaningless in any dispensation where no such safeguard exists.

And that is why such a large chunk of the UDHR is devoted to the vital question of law. The articles assert everyone's right to be treated as a person before the law, equally with all other persons. They state that everyone is to have access to effective remedy for violation of his rights, freedom from arbitrary arrest, and a fair trial – which means trial before an impartial tribunal, a presumption of innocence, and an adequate opportunity to prepare a defence.

The second paragraph of Article 11 says that no one shall be held guilty of doing something that did not constitute a crime at the time he did it; this enshrines a principle of natural justice that was consciously if not uncontroversially set aside in the Nuremberg Principles under which the Nazi war criminals were tried. The Principles defined 'crimes against peace', 'war crimes' and 'crimes against humanity', and were claimed by critics to create a set of '*ex post facto*' ('after the event') offences which no law forbade at the time they were committed. The short answer is that the moral law most emphatically existed – a claim that can be robustly defended, in another time and place – and anyway legal codes and principles everywhere existed which proscribed within their own jurisdictions the kinds of crimes that the Nazis committed, so the Nuremberg Principles were in effect simply an extension and application of them.

But the fact that the Nuremberg process needed a clear articulation of what it sought to condemn is a further illustration, if one were needed, of why Articles 6–11 of the UDHR seemed to their drafters so important: law and its due process lie at the heart of the possibility of rights because without them the idea of rights is in any practical sense empty.

Today's asylum seekers, refugees and displaced persons, and even more so today's legal and especially illegal immigrants, create anxieties in the countries which, because of their wealth and peace, are a magnet to many of them. There is a net flow of people from the south to the north, from Africa to Europe and North America, from the Middle East to Western Europe and the United States. These facts and the real and perceived problems (there are pluses aplenty too) that attend them raise question marks over the UDHR's Articles 13–15, about freedom of movement within and between countries, the right to asylum, and the right to a nationality – and this latter not necessarily of the land where one was born and, perhaps, persecuted.

A principle applied to understanding the UDHR's drafters' intentions and therefore the meaning of the Declarations' articles is a well-established one elsewhere in the interpretation of law. It is: look at the mischief that the provision sought to abate. In the case of Articles 13–15 the mischief was not only the creation of prison-house Third Reich before the victims of its persecution could escape – many did not even try – but the situation in the immediate aftermath of the war, when tens of millions of displaced persons and refugees swarmed in Europe, the Middle East and the Far East, and more were added to their number by dispossessions (for example, of Sudeten Germans by the Czechs), revenge, flight across new borders, starvation, and in many cases the effort to get back to a home that was no longer there – again because of new borders, or as a result of the attrition of war.

It is hard to imagine now the suffering of Europe in the period between 1944 and 1947 when the main collapse of organisation occurred. In China the removal of the Japanese presence gave an impetus to the civil war that ended with the victory of Mao Zedong's Communists over Chiang Kai-Shek's Nationalists in 1949. At first blush it doubtless seems a remote remedy to propose, for the uprooted many in the turmoil of the time, that everyone has a right to free movement, asylum, and a nationality; but if one ponders it, one sees that it is exactly the right organising idea for the crisis, as well as being a right principle in general. For it served as a handrail for decisions about what to do with the displaced and ejected, and in all but one still vexed and inflamed part of the world –

Israel–Palestine – and one recent locus of old bitterness – the former Yugoslavia – it has worked well enough for questions about borders, reparations, and the right of return not to have shed too much blood.

The idea of a right to a nationality is the correlative of the idea of a right to mobility, if one reflects on the matter. An analogy that illustrates the point is this: suppose one could only be allowed a home if one never left it; or that if one were permitted to travel about inside and beyond the borders of one's country, one would not be allowed to go back to the starting point. Obviously enough the idea of having somewhere to go to or return to is key to the idea of travel; it is not travel if one has nowhere to return to, rather it is wandering or lostness. Generalise the point to nationality and movement within and across borders, and – not all that obliquely – one of the drafters' central concerns comes back into focus: that of the minimum conditions for individuals to have a chance of making a good life for themselves. A nationality and the freedom to travel or change one's place of residence and work are framework conditions – not guarantees of flourishing, but necessities even before the work of building a good life can begin.

The articles were drafted in an age when the movements of people occurred largely among neighbours, so that although there is no more acid a conflict than that between people close in language and culture, the chances of assimilation and adjustment are usually far better than when immigration from ethnically, linguistically and culturally remote places occurs and – for entirely natural reasons – immigrants begin to accumulate in one or a few localities. Some arrivers soon move on into the mainstream culture and assimilate; others ghettoize. Plenty of people think that the problems that arise when the latter happens make the ideas underlying Articles 13–15 obsolete, or at least irrelevant, because they were premised on different circumstances. It seems to me that the important questions of immigration, assimilation and multiculturalism do not affect what the UDHR's drafters wanted: which was that everyone should belong somewhere, but not be imprisoned by that belonging.

For quite the wrong reasons, today's readers of the UDHR can get a strong sense of datedness. Article 12 says we have a right to privacy and to protection from attacks on one's honour and reputation. The bright luminous smear that the credit-card-using, emailing, mobile-telephoning possessor of a travel card leaves behind him as he moves about his daily life under the CCTV camera's ubiquitous eye, has made privacy a thing utterly of the past for all but the technophobic drop-out or those beyond a certain age who cannot manage, or be bothered with, the endless fiddlesomeness of getting logged on, registered, connected – and thereafter relentlessly tracked by anyone interested.

In the haste with which we have embraced emailing and mobile phoning we have stripped ourselves naked to any eyes that wish to see. Manufacturers of biometric identity data devices and surveillance equipment have importuned governments into violating the limits of citizen privacy and autonomy by selling them the idea that, by turning every individual into a suspect to be watched and monitored, the tiny percentage of bad folk among them can be caught. There is an irony in this: the bad folk are not always stupid enough to leave a bright luminous smear of their presence on the public record; from the hood to the multiple pay-as-you-go mobile phones, the fake ID and the once-only used internet café, they are going to stay out of reach of that intrusive gaze that watches the rest of us.

Privacy is indeed a right. It is more: it is an essential, as argued earlier. It is a strange and shallow human existence that lives at every moment under the burning eye of the inquisitor – exactly what the Church once wanted us to think was our predicament: existence before the never-closed eye of a jealous divinity, even when we are alone in the dark. It shows that the state, in wanting to attach so many electronic and bureaucratic monitors to its ordinary citizens, has given up on that other idea.

So the UDHR's Article 12 asserts a right that is indeed fundamental, and has already been lost in all practical senses. That does not mean we could not win it back. It does not mean that the injustices which will accumulate in number, and eventually the sheer flood of useless information that bureaucracies will drown themselves in, will not force a retreat. But the privacy principle asserted by Article 12 and other human rights conventions should have stopped it in its tracks in the first place. But then: when principle opposes power, it is too often on the losing side.

What about the right to protection against attacks on one's honour and reputation? Here, too, the brave new electronic world makes this a laughing stock. Look at the blogosphere – the biggest lavatory wall in the universe, a palimpsest of graffiti and execration – to see what a whimsy that idea has become. In jurisdictions like ours, there can be remedy after the fact when such attacks occur in print or on the airwaves: one can sue. For the armies of the anonymous invited to 'post a comment', the only defence would be to compound the felony – by invading their privacy through yet further electronic means. It does us credit if we prefer putting up with them to seeing rights-annihilating power reach into the internet to silence them.

Article 18 not only protects the right of people to have a religion and to change it, but by entailment to not have a religion and to leave the one they were born into. That is a right that would be appreciated by those in dispensations where apostasy can be fatal. Human rights instruments ought to add that people have a right not to be obliged to live according to religiously motivated moralities or scruples that they do not share – a protection against the activities of moralisers who do not wish people to see, hear, read or do what they themselves choose not to see, hear, read or do.

In one sense, of course, one's opinions are inviolable, and will remain so until the day neuroscience produces a machine that can read our thoughts: how some of our liberty-dismantling governments must relish the prospect. They are trying it already, by employing lie detector machines.

But whereas thought is until now free, it is only so if one does not communicate it to anyone. The importance of freedom of speech – protected by Article 19; and which includes, as the jurisprudence of the US's First Amendment shows, all forms of expression – is so great that it cannot be overstated. One accepts, as the discussion earlier shows, that it is not absolute: but the circumstances in which some greater benefit is served by limiting freedom of expression have to be such that, on a strictly individual and one-off basis, an overwhelming case can be made for doing it on that occasion alone. There should, in short, never be a blanket proscription of expression. When such expression is libellous or damaging, there can be remedy after the fact, as when someone sues for defamation. Prior restraint on expression, by contrast, should be a rare and exceptional event. And emphatically, the fact that someone 'feels offended' by someone else's utterances – or cartoons or theatre performances – ought never to be a ground for suppressing free speech. All this was noted earlier in this book, but bears repeating because of its importance.

Articles 18 and 19 speak for themselves. Once again, history abounds with examples of the mischief caused by the absence of these rights. Orthodoxies of belief and political tyrannies, usually hand in hand if not the same thing, have always been profoundly averse to freedom of thought and expression, and indeed have lived by feeding on their corpses. The major example of their lack in the horror years of the 1930s and 40s made it overwhelmingly necessary that an unqualified statement of them should accompany the other aspirations expressed in the UDHR. The language of the articles is unequivocal: rightly so.

For the most ambitious and provocative of the UDHR's aspirations – its assertion that every human individual has social, political and economic rights – the mischief that articles according social and economic rights addressed was vivid in every adult's experience in 1948. Eleanor Roosevelt's husband dealt with the consequences of the crash of 1929 and the droughts of the 1930s: unemployment, hunger, homelessness. Jews were deprived of their livelihoods and lives in Nazi Europe. Many among colonised peoples were without education or a vote. Poverty shut out majorities all over the world from full participation in the political and cultural life of the countries they lived in. The UDHR said that an education, a vote, a decently remunerated job, and access to social goods and opportunities, were rights on a par with rights to life, liberty, privacy and freedom of expression: that is, basic conditions of the possibility of a good life.

The presence of these articles makes it surprising that the UDHR was accepted without dissent by all UN member states. There were grumbles among those who recognised that the articles saying that 'everyone has a right to social security ... everyone has a right to work ... to equal pay for equal work ... to join trades unions ... to rest' implied that these are things that should be done *for* people, rather than – as the earlier articles had it – what should *not* be done *to* people, and therefore seemed to place an obligation on governments to organise matters accordingly. The hand of the NGO members who advised the drafters is visible here: these are activist sentiments, not politicians' sentiments, and they are all the better for it.

What got these tendentious articles through the General Assembly vote, though, was a classic fudge. Eleanor Roosevelt told the Assembly that the US Government 'wholeheartedly supported' the articles, but did not regard them as binding on governments 'to assure the enjoyment of these rights by direct action'. Thus liberated, governments could vote in favour with a sense of self-righteousness. But Eleanor Roosevelt and her fellow-drafters recognised that once the words were inscribed and subscribed, they would serve as an encouragement and a reproach, the goal for those (the activists again) who sought the realisation of those rights, a reproach to those governments who did nothing beyond voting in favour.

Commentators on the UDHR disagree over whether the social and economic rights should be regarded as rights at all. Political rights are a different and more straightforward matter, and the argument is that a successful exercise of these will ensure the social and economic outcomes that the UDHR inappropriately includes. There is a point to this; but it is not the point that the drafters sought to make. Recall the contemporary experience of exclusion, unemployment, hardship, powerlessness: the recent and contemporary reasons for these were various, but they could only be jointly insured against by making education and employment with decent conditions the norm of expectation.

And that is surely right: for what is a right to life, freedom of expression and privacy if one is starving, ignorant, homeless, jobless, disenfranchised? The drafters of the UDHR saw that the idea of the indivisibility of rights has to be taken seriously, and fully embedded in what makes their possession and exercise meaningful. In the liberal democracies of the West since 1948 the circumstances envisaged by the drafters was largely realised in the lives of most ordinary folk, to an extent that has made them (which is to say, us) complacent and inattentive. But to those who lack either the protecting rights (to life, liberty and the rest) or the enabling rights (to work,

education and the rest), the absence of either kind amounts
in practical terms to the absence of all.

Without doubt the UDHR presents itself to sceptical eyes
as a very imperfect document. Among its more obvious
failings are the vagueness of the drafting and its effort to say
too much. But as soon as one recalls that it is a statement
of aspirations, and that it was written in response to the
grievous harm suffered by millions immediately beforehand
during the Second World War, these criticisms can be seen
for the quibbles they are. It is a compendious document – in
the literal sense of 'brief and inclusive' – because its drafters
wished to touch upon all the areas that later documents would
address more explicitly, and to get them agreed by the UN's
member states while sentiment for doing so was fresh and
urgent. The two great Covenants, respectively on civil and
political rights and social and economic rights (both adopted
by the UN in 1966), duly followed, and have the status of
international law. But the document that keeps a hold on the
collective imagination is the UDHR itself, because it is the
one that came hot out of the flames of war, with a directness
of intent and a breadth of ambition that makes it exceptional.
  Critics of the UDHR and of the idea of human rights in
general are of many kinds, but the three chief camps consist
of the complacent, the inconvenienced, and the disappointed.
The first are those who, born, bred and fattened in peaceful
and reasonably sane parts of the world, have the luxury of
cavilling and complaining at will, sometimes arguing that
there is no such thing as a right, that talk of human rights
is variously Eurocentric colonialist arrogance, or hot air, or

pious claptrap, or all three. A few days in a windowless cellar with periodic episodes of water-boarding and electric cattle-prodding would change these minds faster than most.

The inconvenienced range from those who think one man is worth two or more women and therefore do not like talk of equality and rights, to those who have punitive and coercive instincts, and wish not only to lock people up or deport them, but make them suffer extra penalties while doing so, out of revenge and hostility.

The disappointed are those who point to the continuing mayhem, genocides, wars, use of torture and long detention without trial – by would-be respectable Western governments too – and say that fine talk about human rights has made not a jot of difference, and indeed has often served as a fig leaf for abuses.

Of these three camps the third has by far the most cogent point. But what one should draw from it is not defeatism, but renewed determination to make the idea of human rights work. In any case we are, from the long view of history, in the very earliest days of trying to construct a world order, a global sentiment, in which concern for human rights is widespread and operative. Enforcement is the key issue, and here we are in even earlier days: the International Criminal Court, for example, is an infant that does not yet walk. To give up on the idea of human rights now, so soon into the project of trying to remedy the world by its light, would be wrong. Those immediate post-war years in which Eleanor Roosevelt's committee met and debated – its members drawn from the Far East, the Middle East, Europe and America, its lobbyists fresh from the front lines of human suffering – constitute the interpretative background to the UDHR, and if one has that background in mind as one reads the articles, their import comes vividly and urgently across. When that happens, it is impossible to remain indifferent, or to be defeatist. The campaign for human rights is the best hope for humankind, and it would be dereliction not to work to make that hope bear fruit.

As to the second camp's views: its proponents should re-read the UDHR, and especially Articles 29 and 30. Article 29 states that everyone has duties to his community, on which his own possibility for flourishing exists; and they involve 'recognition and respect' for the same rights for others, which is what justifies the existence of a legal and moral social order. The UDHR's drafters did not feel it necessary to labour the obvious point that rights carry responsibilities, that having a claim on others implies that they have a claim on you, that a society of free adults such as envisioned by the drafters has to be a co-operative one, in which rights and duties (not every right has a correlative duty; babies have rights but no duties) are linked.

Article 30 says, 'Nothing in this Declaration may be interpreted as implying for any State, group or person any right to engage in any activity or to perform any act aimed at the destruction of any of the rights and freedoms set forth herein.' All governments – including, alas, the British government, which, having passed a Human Rights Act only to discover that individual liberties are an inconvenience to security services and government aims alike – are one and all guilty of infringing this provision, from Guantanamo Bay to regulations requiring mobile phone companies and email service providers to pass information about all users of their systems to governments.

The need in the United Kingdom, as this suggests, is for something dramatically the opposite of weakening or abolishing the Human Rights Act. The need, instead, is for a written constitution. The disadvantages of such a thing are numerous enough, and in the past the 'constitution of the people', as Voltaire put it, and the traditions of British political life were on balance preferable. That time has passed. It is obvious that our form of parliamentary democracy is no safeguard for civil liberties and human rights, so a defence against their degrading at the prompting of political opportunism, timid statesmanship, vulnerability to reactionary tabloid lobbying, and all the other dangers that constantly besiege liberty, is now urgent.

This reinforces the answer to the third camp of the disaffected. Again: instead of bemoaning the fact that the UDHR era has not yet made enough of a difference, the right thing to do is to work to ensure that it makes more of a difference. The mistake is to be utopian rather than meliorist in one's ambitions for doing so. The utopian seeks for perfection, the meliorist more realistically seeks for improvement. The utopian despairs if perfection proves unattainable, but the meliorist – he who seeks to make things better, incrementally, cumulatively, tirelessly – can take new hope from every success, however small: the political prisoner freed, the military junta replaced by democracy, the tyrant brought to book before a court. In the sixty years since the adoption of the UDHR these things have happened, and they have happened because of the new sentiment it introduced to the world: that is the beginning of something not just better, but good.

PART II
DEBATES

Introduction to Part II

The questions raised in Part I, and other considerations implied by them, are the subject of an extensive debate in the Western world today. In this section I comment briefly on views about them expressed by a number of recent and contemporary writers, among them Isaiah Berlin, Ronald Dworkin, and Tzvetan Todorov, with all three of whom I find much to agree on, and Roger Scruton, John Ralston Saul, John Gray and Slavoj Zizek, with all four of whom I find much to disagree about. Disagreement can be coloured by different responses to the motivations and underlying assumptions of one's opponents' views. In the case of Roger Scruton, I respect some of the impulses that lead him to his outlook, and applaud his gifts as a writer and thinker, but cannot agree with him on substantive matters of principle. In the case of John Gray, I am dismayed both by the methodology and the *trahison d'un clerc* that the formulation and expression of his views involve. This latter is what troubles me about Saul and Zizek too. In the rhetorical battles that lie behind the shooting wars of our time, there is no place for questionable sincerity or the adoption of postures for the sake of notoriety: but it is sometimes hard not to fault those, for this reason, who would like to be thought heretics and who strain hard to adopt the posture of appearing so.

There is a necessary preface to what I say in response to these thinkers, especially to those with whom I disagree. It is to remind ourselves of what is quintessential in all discussions of value, and especially those that are the concern of all the chapters in the first part of this book: the meaning, purpose and content of what are called 'Enlightenment values', for the reason that the historical Enlightenment is the first truly organised moment in mankind's endeavour towards liberty. I start this section, therefore, with an iteration of what 'Enlightenment values' means.

18

Liberty and Enlightenment Values

It is impossible to begin a discussion of what is meant by 'Enlightenment values' without quoting Immanuel Kant. 'Enlightenment,' Kant wrote in his 1784 essay *What Is Enlightenment?*, 'is man's emergence from his self-imposed immaturity. Immaturity is the inability to use one's understanding without guidance from another. This immaturity is self-imposed when its cause lies not in lack of understanding, but in lack of resolve and courage to use it without guidance from another. *Sapere Aude* [dare to know]! Have courage to use your own understanding! That is the motto of enlightenment.'

Neither Kant nor his eighteenth-century contemporaries thought that they lived in an enlightened age; rather, by 'enlightenment' they meant the process of a lessening of darkness, the beginnings of dawn. By the endeavours of the eighteenth-century summation of what had gone before in the struggle for freedoms and rights, for knowledge unconstrained by the control over thought of ancient superstitions, the human mind was liberating itself from traditional authority. 'Nothing is required for enlightenment except freedom,' Kant wrote, 'and the freedom in question is the least harmful of all, namely, the freedom to use reason publicly in all matters.'

Kant and his fellow leaders of Enlightenment were opposed to hegemonies, whether intellectual or political. 'On all sides I hear: Do not argue!' Kant continued. 'The officer says, Do not argue, drill! The tax man says, Do not argue, pay! The pastor says, Do not argue, believe!' Whereas the officer and the tax man serve authorities who dislike anyone questioning the political and social status quo, the pastor is a different matter: he represents the authority that dislikes any kind of questioning, and certainly not the kind that is sceptical about received wisdom.

It is always worth remembering that the Enlightenment's flagship project was the *Encyclopédie ou Dictionnaire raisonné des sciences, des arts et des métiers*, edited by Denis Diderot and Jean le Rond D'Alembert, and published in many volumes between the years 1751 and 1772. Its assault on the authority of religious and political traditions was premised on a recognition of how obstinately they stood in the way of intellectual and social progress. In this the editors and contributors of the *Encyclopédie* were following the lead of Voltaire, whose battle-cry of *ecrasez l'infâme* challenged established pieties and superstition with weapons of satire and reason. 'Have courage to free yourselves,' Diderot exhorted his age in words echoed by Kant, 'Examine the history of all peoples in all times and you will see that we humans have always been subject to one of three codes: that of nature, that of society, and that of religion and that we have been obliged to transgress all three in succession, because they could never be in harmony.'

The Enlightenment was a call to individuals to open their eyes and see themselves and the world by the light of reason. That meant understanding the world through philosophy and science, especially by applying the methods and where applicable the results of both to the social world, education and morality.

The Enlightenment, of course, had its negative aspects and consequences, especially in the counter-Enlightenment reactions to it, represented by those aspects of Romanticism that gave rise to nationalism and racism, and the effort to reassert monolithic tyrannies, especially Nazism and Stalinism as the inheritors of The One Big Truth ideal that was once owned by the Church, and which attempted to reimpose the total authority once claimed by absolute monarchy. But the Enlightenment itself was motivated by a real desire for the improvement of humankind's lot − it was a pluralist, rational, liberty-motivated and above all meliorist, not utopian, project: its adherents had too much good sense and pragmatism to think otherwise − and as such it represents a key moment in the progress of civilisation. Among other things it represents the first dawning of the modern democratic spirit, which would not have been possible without its belief in the universality of the human good and the rights of man.

With these remarks and considerations as background, one is better equipped to evaluate the positions taken by recent and contemporary contributors to the debate in which

questions about civil liberties are a part. A useful place to
begin is with the insights into the concept of liberty itself
offered by Isaiah Berlin.

19

Isaiah Berlin and Liberty

It is easy to miss the point of Isaiah Berlin if you think either that a person's political and moral outlook should accord with an identifiable party platform, or that intellectual achievement is measurable only in bulky monographs. The appearance of something ambiguous, reticent, even uncommitted, in Berlin's thought and public life has misled his critics into thinking he presents an easy target. But they indeed miss the point; for in both Berlin's life and work there is deep consistency and grand achievement.

Berlin was a perceptive historian of ideas, and because he devoted so much attention to investigating the sources of the ideas that have shaped modern times, often in unprecedentedly cruel and destructive ways, he was also a significant contributor to debates in social and political theory. His chosen vehicle was the essay, rich with the distillations of a wide and deeply considered reading, and perfect as the vehicle for his undogmatic, exploratory style of enquiry.

Three interests dominated Berlin's work. One was the history of Russian thought; another was the criticism of the

Enlightenment project mounted by its opponents; the third was the question of liberal values in a pluralistic society. Berlin pursued the first two interests through studies of individual thinkers: Alexander Herzen among the Russians, and Vico, Fichte, Hamann and Herder among the Enlightenment's enemies. He pursued the third interest in its own terms – witness especially his celebrated *Four Essays on Liberty* – but it is pervasively present in his writings on these other topics also.

Berlin held that liberal society by its nature encompasses a plurality of mutually irreconcilable and conflicting values. Most liberals believe that, by tolerance and the exercise of reason, conflicts of values can be resolved and harmony achieved. This is a legacy of Enlightenment attitudes; but these attitudes were premised on the belief that there is a single set of facts about human nature from which values can be derived. The Romantics came to think differently, seeing liberty as the achievement of individual self-creation and self-expression. They therefore repudiated the Enlightenment's universalist conception of human nature – not least because of the terrible implication that some of its inheritors drew, namely, that human nature thus conceived can be improved, despite itself, by those who know best.

Berlin's view is a complex one. He recognised the worthy aspiration in the Enlightenment belief that, by the use of reason, mankind can identify worthwhile goals for itself, and the means to achieving them. He applauded its belief that science and rationality can overcome superstition, despotism, inequality and war. But this faith was strongly opposed by critics who argued that different peoples have different needs and aims, and that there are no universal standards of reason and therefore no ultimate solutions for the dilemmas faced by humanity. Berlin wished to recognise the force of this latter view too, and indeed accepted a version of it. He was therefore committed to the seemingly precarious view that a liberal society is only one form of human possibility, with no special status as against others – but to which, nevertheless, we should commit ourselves. But if liberal society is merely one among a plurality of options, why should we do so?

It is fruitless to try to disguise this tension in Berlin's position, which is never resolved; but one can nevertheless emphasise what is fundamentally worthwhile in it, namely, Berlin's insistence that although by their very nature pluralistic societies are doomed to internal conflicts, it remains worthwhile quietly to push the claims of tolerance as a way at least of managing them. Even if the critics of Enlightenment are right; even if there is an unresolvable conflict of competing values; even if there is no clear answer to how a given dilemma should be resolved; still, says Berlin, tolerance and reason can help to maintain the equilibrium which is, as he put it, the 'first requirement of a decent society'.

If anyone thinks that Berlin's politics – and especially his sense of Jewishness and his Zionism – were equivocal, they will learn from his biographers, among them Michael Ignatieff, why he thought and acted as he did, and see that he kept faith throughout with his own liberal principles. The biographies yield a portrait of a thinker who consistently tried to suggest a way for people to live with one another despite their occupancy of history's most terrible century. His endeavour was, at very least, a brave one. But in the end it has proved an unconvincing one in certain crucial respects, not least in inviting us to accept what in the end threatens every aspect of the liberal project which he sought to defend: the contradictions of liberalism itself.

This is most clearly seen in the failure of the multiculturalist experiment in Britain. The idea behind multiculturalism is that different cultures, creeds and ways of life can peacefully and fruitfully coexist beneath an over-arching tolerance that makes room for them all. It is an admirable ideal, and it works when one or more of the following conditions are satisfied: when the cultural differences in question are not so great, or a minority is adept at preserving its culture in some respects while assimilating well in other respects, or the numbers in minorities remain too small for the differences to be salient or problematic.

In Britain the Jewish community is an excellent example of the first two reasons for success, and the Chinese, Caribbean and Hindu communities are excellent examples of the second and third. Some feel that the South Asian Muslim communities have been unsuccessful in all three because of the third factor – in the sense that the size of the community, with second and third generations having been born in Britain but raised in partially and sometimes significantly separate communities, and with – in turn – resultant feelings of tension between loyalty to those communities and relations with the wider society often involving discrimination or alienation.

In the United States overall social cohesion is maintained by factors as disparate as sheer scale, the wide plurality of ethnic and cultural differences evident everywhere in large cities and on television, the insistence on certain 'politically correct' values of inclusiveness and non-discrimination (it does not of course perfectly achieve either, but the public will towards them strongly exists), and the fact that, despite everything, a certain melting-pot factor does indeed count, at least in the sense that most people who live in the United States sign up to its ideals.

The US is unique in its relative success in these respects. The underlying and now unstated aim is assimilation; the thought is that eventually the population's variety will homogenise over time. In France assimilationism appears to have failed because the otherwise admirable ideal of treating everyone as French and being officially blind to all other differences has meant that communities facing discrimination and deficits in language, education and therefore opportunity were falling further behind and – among their young – becoming restive to the point of occasional violence. In Canada the success of immigration policies has turned on the high bar set for who can immigrate: Canada's immigrants are educated, skilled high-achievers, unlike Europe's immigrants, who when they first arrive tend to be mainly unskilled labourers needed for the tasks that native Europeans no longer wish to do.

All these considerations bear on Berlin's thesis that liberal pluralism is a pluralism of irreconcilable differences that can only be accepted and if possible managed, but must forever exist. The facts appear to suggest that Berlin's picture is a snapshot of a liberal society at an uneasy transitional point on the way to its demise, in the following sense: that the liberal society, for good liberal reasons, welcomes and embraces those who do not quite share its outlook. It tolerates their growth in its midst. The differences become noticeable, then problematic. The liberal society is faced with a choice: require that everyone sign up to shared values, which might well mean some major choices for some or all parties, or drift along with an increasingly problematic situation in the hope that tensions will not turn into conflicts, at least not too soon. By its nature this latter is what liberalism's instincts invite it to do. That it is an unsustainable option is obvious enough; and this thought is what asks for a revision of Berlin's thesis.

For my part, writing as one who locates himself on the liberal left of the political spectrum, I do not accept that a liberal society cannot be demanding – some would say illiberal – in a small number of vital, foundational respects: chiefly, in requiring that anyone who wishes to live in and benefit from membership of a liberal society should be prepared to live by its basic values even as – in conformity with them – he criticises them if he is so moved. This entails that when religious or cultural traditions come into sharp conflict with them, either they must accommodate themselves or yield, or if the espouser of them cannot do either, he must give up membership of the liberal society and seek a place where he can live according to his alternative values. That is a blunt enough statement, to be sure; but consider its application in a test case – that of women. A liberal society is one which is committed to (though so far, in reality, inadequately and incompletely) equality for women in all respects. That means that the rights, choices, opportunities, access to social goods, education, employment, personal autonomy and everything else of value to individuals in a liberal society applies equally and unequivocally to men and women both. Manifestly, such equality is not even accepted in principle in a number

of traditionalist religious communities, such as some forms
of fundamentalist Christianity, some ultra-orthodox Jewish
communities, and most reaches of Islam.

It seems simply implausible that Berlin's view can be
regarded as acceptable in the light of the deep violations of
liberalism's own principles in respects like these. The thought
that one should accept, because putatively one's liberalism
requires it, that girls are undergoing female circumcision and
forced marriages in suburbs of cities in one's own country,
does not persuade. Defenders of Berlin might say that this is
not what he meant; he meant that true liberal principles (of
which female circumcision and forced marriage emphatically
are not examples) themselves come into irreconcilable
conflict, so that a much less extreme, indeed gentler, set of
contradictions are the point, demanding the unending polite
negotiation he seems, in a 1950s tea-time sort of way, to
envisage.

Well: perhaps he did not foresee the kind and degree
of disruption to a liberal polity that its own tolerance and
inclusivity would lead to when what it tolerates is what leads
to or exemplifies certain kinds of intolerance. This fact, which
is the key point in the problem that multiculturalism has run
into – multiculturalism being an arch-liberal ideal aimed at
giving generous room to what is not itself – is the empirical
refutation of his thesis. One laments the fact that this is so;
but it is so.

20

Ronald Dworkin and Liberty

In what is assuredly one of the most important contemporary discussions of liberal values, *Sovereign Virtue* (Harvard University Press, 2002), Ronald Dworkin argues that the three political virtues of liberty, equality and community are not, as so many theorists of both left and right have argued, incompatible with each other, but instead are complementary aspects of a single vision, in which each depends for its realisation upon the existence of the others. That vision now animates the revived states of eastern Europe and parts of Asia, and it was what animated the revolutionary ardours of the eighteenth century. But each of the three virtues has to be properly understood in its own right if we are to see how they reinforce one another, and that is the task Dworkin sets himself. He focuses principally on the concept of equality, currently the least fashionable of the three ideals, and perhaps the most endangered of all species among political concepts.

It is endangered because, whereas centre and left politicians of a generation ago would have been unanimous in claiming that the formation of an egalitarian society is their ultimate goal, that aspiration is no longer part of the left–liberal vocabulary. Such politicians now speak of a 'third way' instead, to distance themselves both from the right's abandonment of individuals to the harsh operations of the market, and the 'old left's' belief that all citizens should share equally in their nation's wealth. But Dworkin points out that the concept of equality which is now rejected was never a sustainable one anyway. It was that every member of society should have the same share of society's wealth as anyone else, irrespective of whether they merited it or not; as Dworkin remarks, such equality cannot be a value because 'there is nothing to be said for a society in which those who choose leisure, although they could work, are regaled with the produce of the industrious.'

Instead, Dworkin argues, equality must be understood in terms of the equal concern for its citizens that any legitimate government must show – 'equal concern is the sovereign virtue of political community: without it government is only tyranny' – and equality of resources or opportunities, giving everyone a fair start in making something of their lives. The two equalities are linked: a government which shows equal concern for all its citizens would work to minimise the kind of disparities in ownership of resources, or access to them, that give some people an unfair initial advantage over others.

To the ideal of equality of resources Dworkin adds that of personal responsibility for making good use of them to create a flourishing life. Each individual has a special responsibility for his or her own life, so even though society has to regard each individual as being equally important in the scheme of things, it cannot be expected to take the place of the individual himself (other things being equal) in the management of his life. Here is where liberty enters, not in conflict with equality but as part of it, as Dworkin defines it, because liberty is as essential a component of equality as equality is essential to the existence of liberty.

One of the most interesting features of the arguments Dworkin deploys is the way they engage with – and oppose – two other famous and influential contemporary views: the value pluralism of Isaiah Berlin, and the liberalism of John Rawls. Berlin believed that liberty and equality are unresolvably in conflict, and that liberal society consists in the constant uneasy negotiation between them. Rawls attempted to base liberalism on the idea of a social contract, allowing questions of political morality to be separated from more general ethical considerations, not least from controversies about the nature of the good life. But Dworkin sees political values as seamlessly part of larger ethical considerations, a view whose full statement requires separate treatment.

One aspect of Berlin's pessimism – for so it is, when his views are extended to the kinds of dilemmas liberal societies encounter when their tolerance has given house-room to intolerance, and their success has attracted those who proceed to cherry-pick its values – that one has to accept is the idea of the continual negotiation between conflicting interests. This is consistent with the more optimistic idea that the values of liberalism are realisable, because it incorporates the historically grounded perception that liberal values are not always simultaneously achievable at different periods of their evolution. That is not a fig leaf for accepting injustices and their perpetuation by arrangements that are difficult to change (not least because of their protection by vested interests). It is rather a recognition that what might be called 'liberal process' – change and adjustment by political debate and the education of social attitudes, democratically and by proper form – is an essential component of working towards the good as liberal values envision it.

Dworkin's view about 'equality of concern' rather than 'equality of share' speaks to the fact of inequalities bequeathed by history to any present moment in the evolution of a liberal society, in which negotiations about readjustments and more equitable (not necessarily equal) dispositions of wealth, influence and other goods are current. It offers a way for the too often slow-moving 'liberal process' to be maximally just, even as it occurs and before the optimal outcomes are secured. It is thus a key idea for defenders of this species of outlook: it identifies a way of potentiating justice in the very business of remedying injustice. And it is an idea that can be married to that of the negotiation on which liberal society depends, not least because it imports the prospect or at least possibility of resolution, absent from the picture painted by Berlin.

Earlier in these pages, discussing the idea of social justice, whose absence or too patchy application underlies some of our present problems, I argue for a version of 'equality of concern' and a recognition that 'equality of share' can be unjust. These points are closely allied to Dworkin's views, which offer a basis in practically applicable ethics for a society whose members have a real chance of making good lives, if the resources for doing so are also to hand.

21

Roger Scruton and
Sentimental Reaction

Roger Scruton's response to the events of 11 September 2001 in New York and Washington was to say in effect that the West's political decadence, by which he means its departure from conservative values of traditional ethnic and religious identity within the nation state, has invited the hostility of the non-Western, and especially Islamic, world. The West's failure to keep its brand of liberty, democracy and secular law to itself, by exporting it along with the globalisation of its economic reach, has, says Scruton, 'plunged the Islamic world into crisis by offering the spectacle of a secular society maintained in being by man-made laws, and achieving equilibrium without the aid of God'. Instead of then saying, '*tant pis* for the Islamic world, which might do better by seeking to profit from the example', Scruton puts the blame on the West itself, for being insufficiently nationalistic and ethnically centred – for being, in short, insufficiently like Islamic countries in those respects.

The fact that the 'non-West' is pouring a huge net flow of actual and would-be migrants into the West, and that a proportion of these many become angry and resentful after arriving in the West because their traditional world view consorts so ill with the values they find there, embellishes the picture correctly painted, Scruton says, by Samuel Huntington's 'clash of civilisations' thesis. The result is predictable enough in Huntington's view: some immigrants to the West have taken it upon themselves to express their resentment by committing mass murder. Scruton's response – that the West should retreat into nationalistic conservatism – surprises by its irrelevance to the problem. Just as one would expect a Jerry Falwell to say that God used 9/11 to punish America for its sins (not least homosexuality), so one expects a right-wing opponent of the European Union, multiculturalism, and other such standard *bêtes noires* of the Right to say that if only we would 'reinforce the nation state' (Scruton's words in his proposal as to what the West must now do), all would magically be well.

Scruton's suggestion is scarcely likely to be welcomed by anyone who advocates democracy, personal liberty and secular institutions of law and education, given that they were long fought for and hard won, and that they are the very condition of the life fully worth living as conceived in the contemporary developed world. Of course, Scruton himself applauds these values too; but his account of how they arose, and how they are to be defended, is strangely distorted. He says that they derive from the Roman imperium, and from the 'self-denial' of Christianity. One might agree that Roman universalism and its conception of law are ancestral to the West's modern political values, but it is perverse to think that they owe much to religion of any form, given that successive attempts at enlightenment have had to struggle vigorously against the repressive tyrannies of dogma and priestcraft, winning relative freedom from them only since the eighteenth century. The good legacy of the eighteenth-century Enlightenment is the set of secular principles central to the Western ethos – personal autonomy, concepts of human rights, the rule of law, democracy – and its bad legacy is the reaction it prompted in the way of political Romanticism, which led to the cancers of nationalism, racism and their joint progeny, militarism, which so blighted the nineteenth and especially twentieth centuries.

There is a paradox at the heart of Scruton's case. He claims fully to recognise the value of individual liberties and democratic institutions, and states that he equally clearly perceives what they owe to traditions of free thought and debate, tolerance, the preparedness to accept doubt, to experiment, and to remain open to fresh ideas – the opposite, one notes in passing, from monolithic orthodoxies that require submission and obedience, and which punish heterodoxy and questioning. (The Church in its heyday, and Stalinism in its heyday, share much in common in these respects.) Scruton sees that the votaries of non-Western faith-based or ethnicity-based communities have to deny these very principles to preserve themselves in being, even to the extent of putting people to death who merely say or think anything at odds with their strict and restrictive orthodoxy. The contrast is between a liberal world view of the kind that has produced free, rich, advanced societies on the one hand, and on the other hand a variety of medieval poverties, chiefly of thought. But instead of standing up for the former and asking why the votaries of the latter do not examine and reform themselves, Scruton asks a different question, namely, Why blame Islam for rejecting 'Western technology, Western institutions, Western conceptions of political freedom, when they, in their turn, involve a rejection of the idea on which Islam is founded – the idea of God's immutable will, revealed once and for all to his Prophet, in the form of an unbreachable and unchangeable code of law'? Some will and perhaps ought to respond, 'Given the very premises of the West which he himself applauds, how can Scruton think that such a question should be taken seriously?'

Now consider these views (expressed in Scruton's *The West and the Rest*) alongside those Scruton puts forward in his *Culture Counts*. There is more to agree with than to disagree with in this latter book, especially as regards the ends Scruton is keen to promote: the maintenance of standards of judgement, and the preservation of valuable cultural achievements – the achievements of 'high culture' – that inform those standards and contribute to the continuance of practical moral and social wisdom now and into the future.

These are good aims, and important ones. In the course of explaining why they matter and what can be done to achieve them, Scruton offers some convincing insights, not least about education. He reminds us that in addition to knowledge of facts and techniques there is also knowledge of how to feel – emotional knowledge – which is required for a just appreciation of the meaning of life and its chief values. The education of our moral sensibilities relies greatly on our capacity to understand, appreciate and appraise the arts, which therefore have to remain central to the curriculum, for they are constitutive of the culture whose preservation and transmission Scruton defends.

And because culture matters in this way, Scruton continues, what is taught in the curriculum has to be regarded as the chief focus of the educational endeavour, rather than the individual thus taught. He sees the failure to get this target right as the cause of dramatically falling standards in contemporary education, which seeks to be 'relevant' to local and temporary concerns through 'student-centred' techniques, thus threatening the loss of that body of cultural expertise and knowledge which is what should be passed on as the sustaining core of society.

It is in this last passage of thought that the transition from what to agree with and what to disagree with begins. First, Scruton describes the West as suffering a 'crisis of identity' (a deplorably reductive concept) caused by multiculturalism within and threats from militant Islam 'without' (here Scruton seems to forget that Islam is one of the West's major religions too). With a gesture towards the one-time importance of Christianity as a sustainer of Western culture, Scruton rehearses the litany of complaints against the relativist, post-modernist, secularist temper of the age as indictable for the 'identity crisis' in question. He is not wrong to say that the first two are to blame for the corruption of the academy, which has made university arts and humanities all but irrelevant to the intellectual life of society; but the very fact that they have done this is evidence that they have not had, because they have not the strength to have, the 'identity destroying' effect he alleges. Outside the academy intellectual life flourishes vigorously, and most of it owes much – whether by direct descent from or reaction to – the cultural valuables that Scruton rightly defends. Accordingly, the trumpet note of imminent collapse with which Scruton begins his book is out of tune and out of place.

This is something inferable, indeed, from what Scruton himself says, when he lists the various ways in which Western art and culture continue not just to survive but to flourish – although his chosen illustrations are without exception conservative, conformist and retrospective: not, as it happens, a bad thing in every case; and in some cases far from it. But the claim about flourishing can be made more generally, not least because there are enough people (the same minority fraction of the population as ever, certainly, but that means in absolute terms a growing number) who care enough about the culture to carry it forward, as such minorities have always done throughout history.

A problem with Scruton's suggestion about how our alleged cultural decay is to be addressed is that he seems to envisage a curriculum dependent on a 'canon', but without – because he does not focus on the problem – suggesting how to prevent the canon from becoming a dead hand on creativity, innovation and fresh thinking, including fresh thinking about old problems. There has to be oxygen in a culture, not just dust-laden stale air. There is no reason why the best of the past cannot be consistent with what is both new and good, but whenever canons lie too heavily across the path of endeavour, it is in danger of being dynamited wholesale out of the way, to general loss.

Perhaps Scruton's doom-saying about the health and identity of Western culture is the sort of thing people say in book proposals on the subject, and then include it in their Introductions because they have already written those dramatic words down and they seem good – especially in Scruton's aphoristic, almost vatic, prose. We all have a tendency to over-egg the pudding in prospect. But there is good reason to think that matters are not as bleak as Scruton paints them. Still, he is right about the importance of culture: and this part of his argument merits notice as an eloquent restatement of that familiar but valid point.

But the overriding point that emerges from both books is Scruton's misperception about the sources of the ethos that made liberal education possible, in opposition to enforced acceptance of an orthodoxy – and historically, a religious orthodoxy. He rightly champions liberal education and the cultural values that it supports, but he cannot have it both ways: there is nothing liberal or educative about stale conformism to the past, nor anything inimical to celebration of the best of the past in the open world that liberal secularism has made possible. This, I think, is the key lesson to be learned from seeing the respects in which Scruton is wrong.

22

John Gray and the Pose of Pessimism

The belief that humans are special and can make progress in a variety of ways is, John Gray says, an illusion, and so therefore are all the systems of thought which have promoted or premised this idea. In *Straw Dogs* this thesis is expressed as the view that since human beings are animals, they are no more capable of directing their collective future or improving their collective lot than are monkeys or marmosets. Oddly, Gray claims that the notions of human exceptionalism and progress originate with Christianity (he appears not to have read Aristotle or the Stoics) and has been inherited by 'humanism' (*par excellence* the descendent of Aristotle and the Stoics), a word to which he attaches at least four separate senses, none of them clear, a fact which explains much of the general difficulty with his view.

The observation that humans are animals is taken by Gray to entail that they are subject to exactly the same determinism as all other animals in respect of population growth and decline, eventual extinction, and impotence in the face of what their 'assemblage of genes' dictates. So, beliefs to the effect that humanity can change itself and its environment, improve its lot, learn from its mistakes, manage its technologies, and strike a balance with the rest of nature, are in his view nonsense. Human fate is dinosaur fate: to exist, and then to vanish, willy-nilly, with humanity having only deluded itself that it understood anything, got anywhere, or achieved anything – least of all in the moral sphere.

In short, the quest for knowledge and the exercise of reason are, says Gray, masks for a false belief in the special status of humankind in the world. As a particular example of this thesis Gray attacks philosophy – the reflective enterprise *par excellence* – as misguided in the past and vacuous now, since in the past it advocated the considered life ('the unconsidered life is not worth living' said Socrates), while now it has neither religious nor political ends to subserve, and is therefore empty.

Let us leave aside the question of why anyone who seriously believed this thesis would write a book about it (the question would be: what is the point? for by its own argument it would change, or at very least improve, nothing), and look at details.

First, consider Gray's use of the word 'humanism'. Originally, in the Renaissance, this word denoted an interest in history and classical philology, and in particular in the works of the classical authors. Because of the content of those studies the term soon acquired its chief meaning, to denote the belief that moral, political and intellectual matters are to be understood and debated in human as opposed to transcendent (that is, religious) terms. Gray appears to be ignorant of this sense, because he persistently claims that humanism results from the belief, which he assigns to Christianity, in the distinctiveness of humanity as against the rest of nature; which puts the cart before the horse, given that Christianity, late in the day – that is, some centuries after Christ, when it was clear that the Second Coming had been delayed *sine die* – acquired the best (but of course not all) of its otherwise slender ethics from classical antiquity, the true source of humanism.

Recently an ignorant use of 'humanism' has made it an alternative to 'speciesism', that is, a belief that the interests of human beings are superior to and always trump those of other animals. Gray frequently confuses this latter use for the second sense already mentioned, in which 'humanism' means that human beings are different from other animals, in the sense of not being part of the animal kingdom. And then he gives it a fourth definition, as 'belief in progress' (this was once more accurately called 'perfectibilism' and was wittily exploded in the satirical novels of Thomas Love Peacock two hundred years ago). Gray's misapprehension about the chief meaning of the word allows him to confuse and conflate the three other senses as need arises.

It takes little to see that recognising that humans are animals does not by itself establish any of the theses Gray says follow from it. Some animals are intelligent, like dogs, and can learn and understand, while others, like worms, seem far more like automata. Humans are somewhere on the scale beyond dogs; Gray's metaphysical determinism applies focally to the worm end of things.

Nor does it take much to see that the three non-standard meanings of 'humanism' Gray uses do not entail one another either. One can hold any one or more of those theses independently of any of the others; they are logically independent. It might seem natural to infer 'humans are more important' from 'humans are different', but consider: we think hamsters are different from humans, without that entailing that they are *ipso facto* more important. Still: if I had to choose between saving a human or a hamster, I would plump for the former, since a human is far more likely than a hamster to have plans, projects, ambitions, relationships of importance to himself and others, responsibilities, things to offer his children and friends, his community, and even perhaps the world at large (suppose he is a Beethoven or Pasteur, which no hamster is likely to be). But this in turn does not entail that I can treat the hamster unkindly. Gray, for a reason not discernable in his arguments, seems to imply otherwise.

Indeed it takes no great biological, psychological, historical or scientific knowledge to see that although humans are indeed animals, they are remarkably intelligent ones, with language and symbolism, who alone in the animal kingdom have invented electric light, television, spectacles, bicycles, cricket, prosthetic limbs, and a million other improvements to life and extensions to human capacities – along with far too many detrimental and dangerous things too, but which are just as much evidence of its unique place in nature as the possession of levels of intelligence and self-awareness greatly in excess of almost all, if not indeed all, other animals. It is silly to think that telephones, dentistry, and CD players are not marks of progress in the relevant respects over how things stood in (say) 1000 BCE or even 1900 CE, even if one does not think the guided missile much of an advance on the spear.

So much for Gray's principal thesis. Its failings become somewhat obscured, however, by other problems in his pages. Here are random examples:

'No one can say what was humankind's original sin, and no one understands how the suffering of Christ can redeem it,' says Gray. One does not have to have had a Sunday School education to know that the sin in Eden was disobedience (relating to the fruit on the forbidden tree), and that the Passion of Christ is supposed to redeem mankind from that and all consequent sin, by being a 'perfect and sufficient' sacrifice for them.

Gray tells the story of an incident in a Nazi concentration camp to prove that there is no such thing as morality. He should read Primo Levi or Tzvetan Todorov, who show the astonishing depth of morality and humanity even in the extreme conditions of the Holocaust, and by extension in the world at large – which, despite all wars and greed, is a theatre of far more kindness, tenderness, affection, and co-operation than of conflict, if the daily life of thousands of years of civilisation-building is anything to go by.

In Gray's *Black Mass* things are appropriately dark. It tells us that the world is in a bad way and that there is nothing we can do about it. Perhaps we can infer from this that Gray's aim is to keep us informed of the true state of affairs, so that we have a reason to feel depressed if depressed we feel; there is, again, no clear point to writing a book on this subject if what it says is true. In a nutshell Gray's argument consists in the repeated assertion that modern secularist thinking is utopian in aspiration, has inherited this aspiration from Christianity, has failed because its belief in progress is false – indeed has, he says, in fact been violently regressive. The only thing that will replace it is more apocalyptic religion-inspired conflict.

One must suppose that there are further points than mere iteration of negativism, which is Gray's preferred and here repeated outlook. The chief of them is that he is against the progressivist ambitions of the secular Enlightenment, and he hopes to annoy its proponents by giving it Christianity for a father and – that weary old canard – Nazism and Stalinism for offspring. What follows goes to certain main points only; a fuller response would consume much paper.

In order to establish that secular, Whiggish (that is, progress-believing), Enlightenment-derived aspirations are the child of Christianity, Gray begins by calling any view or outlook a 'religion'. Everything is a religion: Torquemada's Catholicism, the pluralism and empiricism of eighteenth-century philosophers, liberalism, Stalinism. He speaks of 'secular religion' and 'political religion'. This empties the word 'religion' of any meaning, making it a neutral portmanteau expression like 'view' or 'outlook'. He can therefore premise a gigantic fallacy of equivocation, and assimilate secular Enlightenment values to the Christian 'narrative' of salvation aimed at bringing about a golden age.

For a start, this misreads Christianity, for which truths are eternal and the narrative is a very short one (accept and obey, get to heaven; reject and disobey, do not get to heaven); but more to the point, it misreads the secular view. The secular view is a true narrative of incremental improvement in the human condition through education and political action. Gray thinks that such a view must necessarily be utopian, as if everyone simplistically thought that making things better (in dentistry, in the rule of law, in child health, in international mechanisms for reducing conflict, and so forth for many things) could only have any meaning if it were aimed at realising an ideal golden age. But it does not: trying to make things better (meliorism) is not the same as believing that they can be made perfect (utopianism). That is a point Gray fails to grasp, and it undermines his case. Since that is so, the point bears repeating: meliorism is not utopianism.

But in misusing the word 'religion' Gray blurs and confuses just where important distinctions are required. A religion is a view which essentially premises commitment to belief in the existence of supernatural agencies in the universe, almost always conceived as having intentions and expectations regarding human beings. Such is the myth derived from humankind's infancy, a myth that survives for both institutional and psychological reasons, largely to the detriment of human affairs. Most religions, especially if given the chance, share the totalitarian impulses of Stalinism and Nazism (think Torquemada and the Taliban) for a simple reason: all such are monolithic ideologies demanding subservience to a supposed ideal, on pain of punishment for non-conformity.

Now let us ask whether secular Enlightenment values of pluralism, democracy, the rule of independently and impartially administered law, freedom of thought, enquiry and expression, and liberty of the individual, conform to the model of a monolithic ideology such as Catholicism,

Islamism or Stalinism. Let us further ask how Gray imagines that these values are direct inheritances from Christianity – the Christianity which in its history burned to death any who sought to assert just such values, which sought to censor the world with the Index of Forbidden Books, which coerced and manipulated by excommunications and disabilities imposed on those who would not sign declarations of conformity, and so on and on. It was only in 1828 in England that at last Dissenters and Catholics could do what hitherto only conforming members of the Church of England could do – seek entry to Oxford and Cambridge, stand for Parliament, gain access to many of the social and political institutions and practices without which full participation in the social order was impossible. Indeed, the history of the modern European and Europe-derived world is precisely the history of liberation from the control and impositions of Christianity. I refer the reader to the case for this claim in my full-length discussion of it, *Towards the Light* (Bloomsbury, 2007).

As to the weary old canard about the twentieth-century totalitarianisms, it is astonishing how some fail to recognise them for what they are, namely, quintessentially counter-Enlightenment projects, and ones which the rest of the Enlightenment-derived world would not put up with and therefore defeated: Nazism in seventeen years and Soviet Communism in seventy. They were counter-Enlightenment projects because they rejected the idea of pluralism and its concomitant liberties of thought and the person, and in the time-honoured, un-Enlightened way forcibly demanded submission to a monolithic ideal, just as the religions do when ascendant. They even used the forms and techniques of religion, from the notion of thought-crime to the embalming of saints in mausoleums (Lenin and Mao, like any number of saints and their relics, invite pilgrimage to their glass cases). Totalitarianism is not about progress, but stasis; it is not about realising a golden age, but coercively sustaining the myth of one. This indeed is the lineament of religion: it is the opposite of secular progressivism.

Most of what was achieved in the history of the West from the sixteenth century onwards – most notably science and the realisation of the values listed above – was wrested from the bitter grip of reaction inch by painful and frequently bloody inch. Gray ignores this bald fact of history in order to try to make the modern secular West the inheritor of the ideals and aspirations of what it fought so hard to free itself from (and is still bedevilled by). His, accordingly, is a fantasy version of history. In the face of the central heating that warms him, the modern dentistry that allows him to chew his food, the computer he writes his books on and the airplanes he travels in, he asserts that 'progress is a myth'. But perhaps he does not mean to call material progress a myth, but rather alleged progress in the political condition of a large portion of mankind. Does he thus mean that the movement from feudal baronies to universal suffrage and independent judiciaries is not progress? If it is not, what is it? For it scarcely merits description as regress.

When Gray writes, 'The Bolshevik and Nazi seizures of power were faith-based upheavals just as much as the Ayatollah Khomeini's theocratic insurrection ... The very idea of revolution as a transforming event in history is owed to religion ...' this lumping, exactly where splitting is necessary for clarity, allows him to argue a remarkable circle: the 'secular religions' arose from religion, have failed and were inevitably violent because they were based on myths of progress that required coercion to get people to conform, and now the only thing that can and will take their place is 'the violence of faith' (the violence of the religious religions, I suppose we have to call them now that our linguistic resources have become degraded). So in Gray's view all is mayhem just as all is religion, and we have got nowhere since the beginning of time.

As *Black Mass* progresses it transpires that it is really an extended essay on the Iraq war and why the George W. Bush 'Neocon' project of spreading democracy by the bullet is failing. This was hardly news, and it did not require an upside-down version of modern Western history to say it. Bush's view of the world is a counter-Enlightenment one in its inspirations; the war in Iraq is a replay of an old story that most people in the rest of the world (as Gray does not acknowledge) disapprove of profoundly.

Were there space enough and time here, scores of other points might be made. One example is Gray's claim that Christianity introduced the concept of teleology into Western thought. What of Aristotle's priority here? Another is Gray's assertion that a twelfth-century abbot called Joachim of Flora introduced the idea of the tripartite structure of human history. What about the classical Greek, the ancient Indian, the more than two hundred worldwide versions of the myth of 'ages of mankind' catalogued by historian Giorgio di Santillana? And so on for dozens more instances of error.

But one thing that cannot go unchallenged is Gray's backhanded defence of religion as 'at its best … an attempt to deal with mystery rather than the hope that mystery will be unveiled', and regret that 'this civilising perception' has been lost in the current clash of fundamentalisms. This apology for religion will not do: invocation of mystery has been more a potent excuse for evil than a service to the greater good.

I found one thing almost to agree with: Gray says that politics 'at its best' should not be thought of as a utopian endeavour but as a way of managing circumstances. Yes: and, with good and sensible intentions, to improve them where possible. This last bit is the one that Gray elsewhere seems to suggest is impossible. Thankfully, few but the most depressed share his view.

23

Slavoj Zizek and the Inversion of Values

One paradox of liberalism (in the general, small-'l' sense that denotes a pluralistic society characterised by individual autonomy, free speech and the rest) is that it allows illiberal attitudes and discourses to flourish under its protection. Its principles grant freedom of expression to its own underminers and opponents; it offers impunity and sometimes even celebrity to those who attack it and scorn it from within the safety it gives them. The views it allows its critics to express would in illiberal regimes result in those critics being imprisoned or shot. Those who accept the luxury of being able to criticise a society that does not see itself as entitled to stop them, and who, furthermore, profit from doing so, might fail to recognise the irony; but it is not hard to see why liberal society in fact benefits from its critics. Where all but the voice of authority is silent, that silence – literally as well as figuratively, too often – is the silence of the mortuary.

John Gray is one assiduous critic of the society whose Enlightenment institutions protect and nourish him; another, who might perhaps have better insight into this irony, having direct experience of a dispensation which in its palmier days would not let him speak with the freedom he now enjoys, is the Slovenian sociologist Slavoj Zizek. He is an accomplished exponent of the successful post-modern techniques of paradox, deconstruction and allied methodologies. There is entertainment and insight in this; but there is also a risk for anyone who, criticising the tendency of contemporary liberal societies to make themselves less liberal in their quest for security, thinks that Zizek is an ally in the cause.

To see why he is not, consider his claim that 'universal human rights' are an ideological sham, in effect amounting to 'the rights of white male property owners to exchange freely on the market and exploit workers and women' – a remark that blithely ignores the centuries-long struggle undertaken by working people and women to gain those very rights. The background to his view in this respect is made clear by the argument in his book *Violence*.

Zizek's main argument is that what he calls 'subjective violence' – demonstrators throwing stones and bottles at the police, for example – gets put into proper perspective when we switch viewpoint and see that its background is not a neutral state of peaceful order, but a far greater violence: the 'objective violence' of a capitalist system that is a monster feeding with gross appetite, unconcerned by the harm it is doing to people and the natural environment. This is the 'fundamental systemic violence' which the financiers and businessmen of the World Economic Forum, meeting annually at Davos under heavy police protection, try to persuade themselves and us is in our interests. And, Zizek further argues, the leading figures among capitalists – people like Bill Gates and George Soros – go further and commit themselves to vast acts of philanthropy to prove the point: but their humanitarian mask conceals the face of exploitation that brought the surplus wealth into their philanthropic hands in the first place.

For Zizek, the philanthropists, whom he oddly calls 'liberal communists', are therefore 'the enemy of every progressive struggle today'. Terrorists, religious fundamentalists and corrupt bureaucrats are merely local figures in contingent circumstances, minor in comparison to these true enemies of progressive endeavour, who are the embodiment of the system that is itself the true violence in the world. 'This needs to be borne in mind,' Zizek writes, 'in the midst of the various tactical alliances and compromises one has to make with liberal communists when fighting racism, sexism and religious obscurantism.' Given that Zizek rejects notions of rights and liberties as a conspiracy by capitalists to disguise their true objectives, it is hard to see what the motivation would be to fight against racism, sexism and religious obscurantism – for usually the justification for opposing them rests on the significance of those very same rights and liberties.

Zizek also applies his analysis to media coverage of crime and unrest, and the use made of fear by governments and media to motivate attitudes in societies that think of themselves as liberal and tolerant without actually being so. Talk of crime and unrest, and raising fears, are, says Zizek, part of capitalism's conspiracy to make us think that we are well served by notions of liberties and rights. If we reject capitalism we must reject the façade of these notions too.

The key problem in Zizek's argument lies in its premise.

It consists in an all-important equivocation on the word 'violence' which he uses to describe what he takes to be the true nature of liberal societies. One can illustrate the problem as follows:

One can, and should, complain vociferously about the harms and wrongs perpetrated by capitalism, but to describe them all as violence makes it impossible to distinguish between what happens when a multinational oil company raises its prices and when it pays to have people bullied off the land beneath which oil deposits lie. Being paid a low wage and being shot in the head are two rather different things, and sometimes the former is the lesser evil of the two. If one uses the same word for both one is muddling, weakening and misdirecting the argument.

This is what underlies the discussion in Zizek's book, and it is why the discussion is not about the difference between the relatively infrequent situation in which, say, a small number of religious fanatics carries out acts of mass murder, and the standard situation in a Western liberal democracy in which security forces, existing at the implicit and occasionally explicit desire of most of its citizens, are maintained to enforce laws arrived at, and changeable by, non-violent political processes.

The least plausible idea in Zizek's analysis is that the response to the systematic 'objective violence' of the dominant ideology in the West and its institutions, namely global capitalism, is – quite literally – to do nothing. 'The first gesture to provoke a change in the system,' he says, 'is to withdraw activity, to do nothing ... the threat today is not passivity, but pseudo-activity, the urge to "be active", "to participate".' This is not consistent with Zizek's other assertion, quoted earlier, that to oppose racism, sexism and religious obscurantism one has to 'compromise' with the system, for to do any of these things is to be active, and to participate; revealingly, the system's efforts to oppose these things have to be 'compromised' with because they are tainted – presumably they are 'bad' opposition to racism and the rest, whereas non-capitalist anti-racism is 'good' anti-racism.

But such a view is altogether too precious. In a pluralistic society where, by the very nature of its pluralism, interests compete and conflict, those who are concerned about its fundamental values have to fight on many fronts at once: against the system when it encroaches on liberties, against the individuals or groups who misapply those liberties for ends that interfere with the interests of others (e.g. using free speech to try to curtail the free speech of others), and on behalf of the good, whatever its shape and local name. The idea of the disengaged intellectual – Zizek's do-nothing complainer – is a deeply unappealing one, and lends weight to the distrust and suspicion that transfers to the intellectual's stock in trade, which is ideas. Moreover, ideas themselves are empty vessels unless applied, tested, and connected with practice.

Zizek describes himself as a follower of a school of thought that mixes the views of Marx with those of the psycho-analyst Jacques Lacan. It is odd that Marxist intellectuals – now an almost extinct species at least in the political sphere – should of all people have forgotten Marx's strictures on the topic of *praxis* and *gnosis* (practice and theory), namely, that the real task we face is to change the world, not just to describe it.

But it might of course be that there is another, unexpressed, view behind Zizek's advocacy of passivity. If we do nothing to deal with the crisis in liberal society, it could fail and accordingly transform into another kind of society, either more congenial to Zizek's views or more amenable to further change, perhaps by compulsion, into such a society. The historical examples of political systems that conform to some extent with Zizek's views, though, are extremely unattractive; they all in practice had to borrow the dress of authoritarian arrangements hostile to variety, multiplicity, free speech, consent and institutionalised protections for associated rights. Zizek sees the societies currently premised on these things – liberal democracies – merely as fronts or masks for capitalist interests, but this is to confuse two things: the libertarianism that capitalist interests always promote, and the liberal ideals that oppose the exploitations that libertarianism leads to. Confusing them is a basic error.

For present purposes the point is that whereas Zizek is right to point an accusing finger at the power of capitalist interests and the harm they do – to individuals, to the environment, and in causing disasters like the credit collapse of 2008 – he is wrong to see the hard-won dispensation of civil liberties and rights that define Western societies as mere disguises behind which those interests lurk. Just two, though important, examples show why: trades unionism and forms of social democracy are beneficiaries of the Enlightenment settlement as much as capitalism itself, and capable of constraining it and delivering great advantages in doing so.

That is another reason why they merit defending. It is certainly a reason for arguing that a critique of capitalism

24

John Ralston Saul and
Voltaire's Bastards

Western civilisation is in crisis, so John Ralston Saul claimed in his book *Voltaire's Bastards*, because we believe in reason. We live in thrall to a utopian ideal of rational society, first mooted by Enlightenment thinkers in the eighteenth century; but the result, contrary to Voltaire's hopes, has not liberated humanity but enslaved it to a bureaucratic corporatism which stumbles, unconstrained by moral purpose, from one disaster to another.

In stating this theme Saul anticipates by a decade John Gray's rather similar stance of defeatism and negativity about the idea of Enlightenment, the values it stood for and the progress it has inspired. Together Gray and Saul represent a school of a thought which, since it represents the West attacking itself, has to be considered a sort of intellectual auto-immune disease. Using the freedom of speech, the education, the opportunity to get information, the technological appurtenances provided by the scientific revolution, and other advantages stemming from the success of the Enlightenment, they attack the Enlightenment; and of course are entirely free to do so, even though if they lived in a non-Enlightenment-enabled state they would not be permitted to criticise it, and might suffer if they tried.

Not, of course, that everything Saul and Gray have to say is without point. Saul's thesis is that Enlightenment philosophers sought to rescue people from the arbitrariness of royal or priestly power and to replace it with rule by reason. But their dream collapsed because of reason's own limitations. All that happened was an increase in influence of technical elites. The world, in short, became the fiefdom of *managers*. Owners of capital do not control capital; voters do not control politics; everything is run by managers who alone know how to manipulate the structural complexities of society. And the managers' goals – profits, election victories – are not shaped by morality.

This theory of technocratic corporatism – familiar in outline from the writings of the Frankfurt School and other sources – is made by Saul to apply as much to the recently collapsed Eastern bloc as it does to the West. Indeed the East–West distinction, like that between Left and Right, is not a real distinction at all, Saul argues, but a fiction of the managerial strategy by which the Age of Reason sustains itself.

There are indeed some good observations here, but also some not so good inferences and conclusions. Simply by listing the problems of contemporary civilisation anyone can make telling points. Politicians, Saul reminds us, get away with speaking nonsense because what counts is the manner not the content of their utterances. Governments brazenly continue despite their failures because the concept of responsibility no longer applies. Television, advertising, and the worship of artificial heroes such as soap-opera and film stars blind people to the world's predicament.

These phenomena, and many besides, are symptoms of malaise. Worse still are such examples as the arms trade, encouraged by governments who make pious pronouncements about peace and freedom, but who subvert both by their participation in what is effectively gun-running. And this is only part of a story in which 'military-industrial' establishments (against which President Dwight D. Eisenhower famously warned) flourish, and in which many parts of the world are perennially engulfed in conflicts that use the weapons they produce.

Particularly telling support for Saul's thesis comes from the collapse of the world financial system in 2008, in no small part because of the under-regulated greed and folly of money men on Wall Street, in the City of London, and elsewhere, whose cupidity if not dishonesty plunged the whole world into recession.

Although Saul's compendium of problems contains nothing new, his restatement of them serves to keep us alert. But he misdiagnoses the sources of the problems, and overstates them, with the result that the argument soon ceases to persuade, not least because it lays all the blame on one ill-defined abstraction, 'reason'.

At first Saul claims that reason cannot be defined, and then proceeds to define it. Reason is, he says, an obsession with truth and falsity. It is also an obsession with efficiency. It expresses itself in 'control of structures' and as the technique of finding 'simple and absolute' solutions to problems. It is essentially technocratic. Worst of all it is amoral and blind.

This is illustrated by the fact that 'the murder of six million Jews was a perfectly rational act'. It has led to managers, corporatism, and almost everything objectionable in recent history.

These claims will not do. For one thing, blame for the world's problems rests not with a concept but with people. Reason is merely an instrument which, correctly employed, helps people draw inferences from a given starting point without inconsistency. Choosing a sound starting point is what matters. Blaming 'reason' is as meaningful as blaming 'memory' or 'perception'. It was the racism and especially anti-Semitism of Nazis, not the logic they applied to put their hatred into effect, that chiefly caused the Holocaust.

Can Saul mean that the use of reason is bad without qualification? Once again I imagine him sitting before a laptop, answering the telephone, taking antibiotics for his sore throat, flipping switches to get warmth and light as cold night falls. Are all these products of reason contemptible?

The problem in Saul's argument appears when we examine his alternative. Early on he says the opponent of reason is 'reasonableness', which 'practical humanists' such as Jefferson possessed. This is mere wordplay, if not contradiction. But at the end of the book we get a list of virtues to put in reason's place. They are 'spirit, appetite, faith, emotion, intuition, will, experience'. One immediately notes that all but the last, if ungoverned by reason, are exactly the stuff that fuels fanaticism and holy wars. Saul offers them as a solution to the technocratic corporatism that he thinks reason produces; but they are the problem reason tries to solve or at very least contain.

What is needed here is a richer conception of the work done by the concept of reason in Enlightenment thought. Two of the Enlightenment's leading figures, David Hume and Immanuel Kant, offered critiques of reason to illustrate a contention central to the thought of both, that unconstrained *a priori* reasoning of the kind associated with Rationalist theories of knowledge – which argue that truth can only be arrived at by rational excogitation from self-evident first principles or 'innate ideas' – are inadequate, and that reason has to be married to and constrained by experience, in particular to empirical enquiry as exemplified by the natural sciences. The ideal of Enlightenment enquiry is applied reason; the argument in the eighteenth-century theory of knowledge was an argument about the sources of authority over our view of the world and humanity: is it to be tradition, ancient doctrine, the teachings of a priesthood, or is it to be enquiry, experiment, investigation, and the reasoning that is responsible to all three?

This is where Saul's mistake about 'reasonableness' lies. Paradigmatically, Enlightenment reason is indeed reasonable; it is the proportioning of evidence to belief, the recognition of practical limitations, acceptance of the 'crooked timber of humanity', a belief in meliorism and optimality rather than utopian perfectibilism. This does indeed imply a form of managerialism for organising society's daily affairs, but not of the totalising kind that Saul, following the Frankfurt School, claims is what resulted in Nazism and Stalinism: for whereas the pragmatism of the Enlightenment turns to pluralism, personal autonomy, impartial legal process, the idea of inviolable individual rights, and the concomitant need for

25

Tzvetan Todorov: Hope and the Good

Tzvetan Todorov's characteristically rich and insightful *Hope and Memory: Reflections on the Twentieth Century* is, among other things, about the nature and uses of historical memory, and about the significance of individuals who face historical cataclysms with the special attitude Todorov calls 'critical humanism', and by doing so carry the light of the best human possibilities through the darkest times.

Todorov's ambitious aim is to survey the titanic clash between totalitarianism and democracy in the twentieth century, and then to examine the place of memory and history in making sense of that clash — not just from the perspective of the aforementioned lessons, but of how memory and history were themselves manipulated by the century's totalitarianisms, one point of doing which is to remind ourselves that both memory and history have many uses and can be applied in many different ways.

The book was written before the events we now refer to as 9/11, but Todorov has since added a supplementary preface to the paperback edition in order to bring the atrocities of that date within its scope. Interestingly, the book gains from having been written outside the shadow of those events; as Todorov was writing it the pressing contemporary concern was Kosovo, which therefore occupies a substantial part of the book's horizon, but with valuable lessons of its own to impart. The book's primary focus is Europe in the twentieth century, whereas 9/11 was an American and global event for the twenty-first century; but Todorov shows that for America the memory-lesson of that event is the same as for Europe or anywhere and any time else: that 'we learn more from our mistakes than our good deeds. Thanks to them, we can begin to moderate pride with humility – and to see that, very often, the best way of defending our own interests lies in not neglecting the interests of others.'

Todorov begins by discussing the nature of both totalitarianism and democracy and the conflict between them, and then turns to the related topics of memory and history. Between the discussions are digressions on the six 'critical humanists' whom Todorov applauds as emblematic of the human spirit's resistance to the century's evils: the Russian-Jewish writer Vasily Grossman; that extraordinary witness of the century's oppressions, Margarete Buber-Neumann, who was imprisoned by both the Nazis and the Soviets; the French writer and campaigner David Rousset, whose experience of concentration camps under the Nazis later led him to campaign against the Soviet Gulag; Primo Levi, the Italian poet and novelist of the Holocaust; the brilliantly insightful French novelist Romain Gary; and the camp survivor and Algerian War campaigner Germaine Tillion.

For Todorov, a humanist or 'critical humanist' is a philosopher of democracy, and therefore a pragmatist. Humanists know that no knowledge can ever be claimed as final and definitive, and therefore no '-ism', including 'scientism' (the belief that science will explain everything and solve all problems), is going to yield final answers and bring heaven to earth. Instead, humanism is an attitude premised on the principle that all people have the same rights, and the same claim to respect, no matter whether or not they live in the same ways as each other. There will be no paradise on earth because there is evil in man and the world; but these things are 'of one substance' with human life because they arise from our freedom to choose. But human sociability and incompleteness can lead us to cherish one another, which implies a refusal to treat one another merely as means to ends. Of course, the ever-present risk that people will prey on each other rather than cherish each other means that there can be no Utopia, no global and ultimate solution to the problems of human existence. But at least humanism invokes the hope that people will see and treat others as individuals, not as objects or mere label-bearers of one kind or another; and in that belief lies the best hope for mankind.

In his earlier writings Todorov described the human realm as an 'imperfect garden', and he constantly reprises this view. His humanism is down to earth, pragmatic, and sometimes even world-weary; it does not sing mankind's praises without qualification, because it recognises its failings and its capacity for evil. But it is not pessimistic, for it acknowledges that through their capacity for freedom of choice people are also capable of cherishing each other; and that is their salvation, so

far as salvation is possible. This is why humanism has affinities
with democracy, because the humanistic impulse towards
community and fraternity give individuals their best chance
of flourishing.

That is one worthwhile lesson Todorov draws from his
examination of the twentieth century. The other concerns
memory itself. Our choice is not between remembering or
forgetting the horrors of totalitarianism, he says, because
forgetting is not something we can do by an act of will.
Rather, the choice is between different ways of remembering.
The kind that can best help in facing the future neither
trivialises the past nor makes it sacred in some way. What
memory of the twentieth century, thus viewed, teaches is
that democracy (or humanism: the terms are convertible in
Todorov's lexicon) faces three dangers: too much identity
politics, too slavish an adherence to 'moral correctness', and
'overinstrumentalisation' in the sense of too great a focus
being put upon means rather than ends. Overcoming these
three dangers does not guarantee individual flourishing, but
is a necessary condition for it; and a focus on individual
flourishing is itself the best defence against a return to the
totalitarian horrors of the last century. In these remarks can
be seen the necessary correctives to views such as those put
forward by Gray, Saul, and Zizek.

In his *Imperfect Garden: The Legacy of Humanism* (Princeton,
2002) Todorov describes humanism as consisting in a
commitment to believing that individual liberty, personal love,
and a sense of belonging to a moral community, can bring
mankind happiness (even if only 'fragile and fleeting') and –

more importantly – the opportunity to live in truth. Moreover, it can do this without the need of gods or Providence. His book is a sustained defence of this commitment against the charge that what it involves carries an excessively high price – the price, namely, of destruction of all values and relationships, and ultimately of the self itself.

Todorov dramatises these claims as a Faustian pact. The allegory goes as follows. The Devil offered Modern Man free will, which means the power to choose how to live. But he hid from Man the triple cost of this gift, which was that it would separate him from God, from his fellow man, and finally from himself. God will vanish because there will no longer be reason to believe that there exists a being superior to man, and therefore man 'will have no more ideals or values – he will be a "materialist"'. Fellowship will go because other people will no longer matter, and every individual's circle of concern will shrink from community to family and in the end to his own self. And finally the individual's self will go too, because once separated from his community an individual will be nothing but a collection of impulses, 'an infinite dispersal', alienated and inauthentic.

Obviously enough this account holds no water, and the main point of Todorov's argument is to demonstrate why, principally by showing that humanism does not have to purchase the freedom it takes as its fundamental premise – the freedom of the individual – by forfeiting common values or social relations, nor by sacrificing the integrity of selfhood. He does it by looking at the statement of the humanist case in its inception, in the full vigour of its originators' thought, which in his view occurred in the period from the sixteenth to the nineteenth centuries, with

Montaigne, Descartes, Montesquieu, Rousseau, Constant and Tocqueville in its vanguard.

Through discussion of these writers Todorov formulates his own conclusions. These are that humanism involves three principal theses: recognition of the equal dignity of everyone, altruism (the 'elevation of the particular human being other than me as the ultimate goal of my action'), and the preference for freedom of action. These are irreducible values, he says, in the sense that they cannot be explained in terms of each other; they may even indeed conflict at times. But what creates humanism is their interaction, principally through the way they constrain one another. My freedom cannot be enjoyed at the expense of your freedom or dignity; my autonomy is limited by considerations of the equality and fraternity of all in the community to which I belong. Citizens might be interchangeable as members of society, but as individuals they are irreducible; it is their differences that matter, not their equality; and the relations between them turn on preferences and love.

Todorov describes the human domain as an 'imperfect garden' because this humanism is pragmatic and realistic. Humanists do not 'believe' in man or unqualifiedly sing his praises. They see his failings, and they know his capacity for doing harm. But through his freedom he is also capable of choosing the good, and this saves him. The values of community and relationship are voluntary, and at their best humans premise their lives on them. In this respect humanism has natural affinities with democracy, even if it does not single out one political persuasion rather than another; for the humanistic impulse towards community and fraternity reveal that its basis is the belief that others, far from being Hell, are our escape from Hell – which, although it does not make the human realm Heaven, at least makes it fully man's own.

There is much in these views, and their presentation, to admire and accept. Todorov makes a persuasive case for a kind of secular ethics without illusory ideals of the starry-eyed kind. His pragmatic, phlegmatic, experienced view of things human reminds one of the same mature view as expressed in the poetry of Horace – and for that reason recommends itself as a corrective to the enthusiasms which strain towards utopian visions of the good, visions which find proofs of mankind's large capacity for evil – for an egregious example, the Holocaust – difficult to contain and assimilate.

But although I sympathise with almost all of what Todorov says, I have a minor cavil about the way he gets his argument going. This is that the supposed cost exacted by 'the Devil' for man's free will is, as Todorov describes it, immediately and obviously implausible. In the end, of course, that is Todorov's point too; but he makes it seem as if there is a real problem to solve. Yes, the notion of supernatural agencies crumbles to dust when mankind attains his majority and assumes moral and intellectual responsibility for himself, because of course varieties of fatalism, and subordination of the self to heteronymous direction which most religions demand, evaporate. But this happens in conjunction with views of the natural and social worlds informed by science, among them observations of the essential sociability of humankind; so that at the very outset of adopting his autonomy and individuality, modern man recognises his needs and obligations as a social being too. That is why the humanist project of the Enlightenment immediately involved debate about institutions of law and government, and practices of education and morality, of the kind required to enhance and sustain a community of freely though mutually engaged agents. So centrally is this fact placed in humanism that it is hard to see how opponents, supposititious or otherwise, could have failed to recognise the essentially democratic and contractual nature of the ideal.

The real problem faced by the humanist project – which incidentally I think has existed, in ways very similar in content though slightly different (because of historical factors) in form, from classical antiquity onwards, in long-running conflict with religious outlooks – is the continued strength of anti-humanistic influences, chiefly the continuation and in many places dominance of religious ideologies and the traditionalist societies they produce, in which women are second-class citizens and modern science, education and law are suppressed if they conflict with orthodoxy of belief.★ Todorov gives an illuminating overview of the alternatives to humanism in his conclusion, and alludes to the difficulty they pose to the humanist case. But what counts even more is an understanding of the fundamental differences between the premises involved, for it is they that give rise to the struggle, in the past (and still in the present) frequently dangerous and bloody, that people continue to face; for their freedom from old ghosts is not complete, and the liberty, love and community which Todorov eloquently describes remain prone to blight while that is so.

★ I enlarge on this in *What Is Good?* (Weidenfeld, 2001)

26

History and Progress in the Twentieth Century

History is accelerating, chiefly because the speed of communication is increasing exponentially, and communication is a powerful fuel. Everything – travel, political decisions, the exchange of information, the inception of war, deals and trades in the world's markets, discoveries in science and medicine and their effects on human societies – happens so much more rapidly than ever before that it is as if a contemporary hour equals the years or even decades in which most earlier history unfolded. Then events moved in long, slow ripples of change; now they fly in a blur. As a result, it takes vastly more ink to write a history of modern times than a history of some period in antiquity, and not simply because the quantum of available data is greater. Time itself has changed: it is fuller, it veritably bursts at the seams with tumult.

This is even more the case when the history in question is not merely a relation of kings and wars, the stuff of standard textbooks, but a narrative of ideas in art, science, literature and politics, and their complex interaction in weaving the fabric of events. To attempt such a history for modern times is a bold and ambitious project indeed, demanding much of the writer who ventures it, and offering much to the reader if he succeeds. It is not only ambitious but necessary, because a narrative that orders the multiplicity of the twentieth century's thought-world promises to reveal its patterns, and thus to help us make sense of it. If any century requires to be made sense of, it is the tragic, amazing, swift-flying twentieth century.

Science is one of the main keys to understanding the twentieth century. It is scarcely believable that at the century's beginning man had yet to manage powered heavier-than-air flight, was only just beginning to understand the internal structure of the atom, was still virtually powerless against microbes, and mostly believed that knowledge was in essentials complete. Less than half a century later the first atomic weapons exploded over Hiroshima and Nagasaki, dropped by long-range bombers, and some of the survivors were treated with penicillin. Anyone who had lived through the mighty changes thus expressed would have been even more amazed by the difference between the code-breaking machine at Bletchley Park where Alan Turing worked, and the super-computers that now run most of the advanced world.

The twentieth century was an odd place, all the more so for the changed dimensions of its preoccupations and tragedies that retrospect affords. It is entertaining to learn that a newspaper so disliked Schoenberg's music that it reviewed his Second String Quartet in its 'Crimes' section, and that when T. S. Eliot replied 'my entire corpus' to a reporter who asked what he had been awarded the Nobel Prize for, the reporter's next question was, 'When did you write that?' To get a sense of the century one has to go from the intricacies of quantum theory to the history of the modern formation of the Middle East, from the literary and artistic *annus mirabilis* of 1913 to the philosophy of Richard Rorty and W. V. Quine, from the discovery of DNA to the 'culture wars' of recent America – and so on to all the other personalities, events, discoveries, comedies, tragedies, wars, atrocities, revolutions, and natural and human catastrophes on scales unprecedented because the technologies for them, and the population sizes to be affected by them, made them impossible until the twentieth century telescoped time and filled it with a thousand times more of everything.

If we need to read history to make sense of ourselves, the need to read the twentieth century's history is imperative. Even though futures are rarely exact replicas of pasts, they can too often be infected by them. That is one of the chief reasons for undergoing the disinfectant process of knowing as much about our tumultuous past century as we can.

And this is why the preceding chapters have canvassed the ideas of some of those who have responded to the twentieth century with theorising about the state of humankind and society. There are those who say that history teaches no lessons, because the present and future are too different for any such lessons to apply; and there are those who more pertinently point out that to ignore the lessons of the past is to be condemned to repeat them.

An assumption of the first view is that the passage of time merely by its nature is an agent of wholesale change, implying that if we had discovered something of significance at some

point in history – the Enlightenment values, for example –
the march of history soon renders them irrelevant because
out of date. This is a convenience for those who think that
the availability of new technologies of policing, surveillance
and control should be employed because history has moved
on and their existence, together with the real and supposed
threats their use might hope to counter, is justified by that
fact.

But I wish to argue that the ideas which emerged in
the eighteenth century about individual autonomy and
rights, pluralism, a framework of impartial law impartially
administered, privacy, freedom of thought and expression,
democratic institutions, secularism, and the importance of
education and equality of opportunity, are achievements
of history that should be permanent because the principles
and ideals they embody are universal and right. The post-
modern world view with its scepticism about universal
principles, and the opposition of mindsets that also claim
universality and permanent truth but for ideas originated in
much earlier phases of human history (in blunt truth: among
unlettered and ignorant tribesmen), and now maintained
in the self-interest of their inheritors, constitute the main
obstacles to what the Enlightenment project seeks to realise
in the way of liberty and rights for all.

To those obstacles must now be added the actions of the
governments of advanced countries in dismantling the civil
liberties that Enlightenment endeavour largely achieved. If
this process is not successfully opposed, people will see this
time in our history as a watershed; the brief flourishing of free
societies will no doubt be regarded as a bad thing, and blamed

for the excesses that brought them to an end; it is for that reason, among others, that one wishes to register a protest against that rewriting of history, if it occurs, even if it means using one of the last opportunities of freedom to say so.

27

Justice at Last?

Almost everyone engaged in the field of human rights welcomed the treaty, signed in Rome on 17 July 1998, which established an International Criminal Court (ICC) aimed at bringing to justice individuals responsible for 'crimes against humanity' such as genocide and ethnic cleansing. The American commentator David Rieff did not welcome the ICC; he argued that it is the wrong answer to the political and moral challenges posed by such crimes, and said that it will merely prompt disillusionment because, like its sponsor the United Nations, it will be yet another international institution that promises far more than it can deliver.

Rieff's argument in support of this pessimistic view was based entirely on the practical difficulties that everyone knew the ICC would be likely to experience in bringing offenders to justice, with the corollary that its existence will therefore have no deterrent effect on prospective perpetrators of crimes against humanity. Rieff accordingly argued that there is no practical alternative to force as a means of stopping the kind of thing that happened in Bosnia and Rwanda in the 1990s –

and in his view the only available provider of the right kind and degree of force is US military might. And he pointed out that although the ICC is limited in its competence (when it was formed, known human rights criminals such as Augusto Pinochet and Saddam Hussein lay beyond its reach), it interfered enough with national sovereignty to alarm those in the USA who prefer isolation. If they have their way – so Rieff's argument implied – the only effective practical means of international policing would accordingly be undermined.

In the pages of London's *Prospect* magazine I debated these arguments with Rieff. The questions at stake remain of the first relevance, and the debate likewise retains its value as marking what was thought and hoped at the outset of the new institution. In defending it, I wrote in response to Rieff as follows:

Dear David Rieff: I agree that the ICC's constitution, and the contemporary state of the world, together present formidable practical obstacles to its effectiveness. But that is no objection to its existence and the hopes that it offers for the future. Establishment of the ICC is not a panacea; tyranny and murder are not going to stop because it exists. But its establishment is a highly important step, if only one step, in a journey that began with adoption of the Universal Declaration of Human Rights in 1948 – a short enough time in historical terms. The Universal Declaration and its two associated Conventions are now widely influential in both international and domestic jurisdictions. Everyone has been conscious of the need for these instruments to have teeth; the ICC is the first big step in realising that goal. As a culture of law in the international arena grows, so the ICC, and the means for making it an effective body commanding respect and co-operation in the world community, will grow too.

The point I think you miss concerns the principle underlying the concept of an ICC, and the medium and long-term aspirations it embodies. In fact it's hard to believe anyone can disagree with the principle of the ICC, namely, that there should be for the world community what any civilised national community has, viz. a peaceful, rational, properly constituted means of dealing with crime and wrong. The trials at Nuremberg and Tokyo after the Second World War provided precedents for bringing individuals to justice for violations of human rights, but those tribunals, and the one currently in operation for Bosnian crimes, are *ad hoc*: a permanent and properly constituted institution for these same purposes is obviously preferable.

At no point has the sole or even the chief claim of the ICC's advocates been that its existence will prevent all crimes against humanity, although it will certainly prevent some – one should not underestimate the deterrent effect on a would-be Pinochet or Pol Pot if he thought that, at some stage, he could be called to account before an international tribunal for what he does. But more importantly, it offers the alternative of justice in place of revenge for wrongs done; it offers the possibility of redress to those wronged; it offers an important contribution to processes of healing and reconciliation after conflicts, something not always possible without the execution of justice on behalf of victims or their relatives; and it offers a chance of truth, or something anyway better than rumour and legend, in the record of conflict and crime in tragedies like Bosnia and Rwanda.

Your objection to the ICC on the grounds of the practical difficulty it faces is rather like objecting to Montgolfier's balloon because it is not (yet) a Boeing 747. Have patience: just as the introduction of law to the Wild West was (so Hollywood tells us) a hard slow process, so much more is the process of making the international arena a lawful domain. That is a noble aspiration, and putting in place the first concrete measures for its realisation is not a short-term task. Since the international arena is a lawless place, you say, there is no point in trying to apply law to it. Would Wyatt Earp have accepted such an argument?

The debate about the ICC has prompted objections you either do not emphasise or do not mention. Some commentators object that, despite the principle of complementarity embodied in the Rome Treaty (which provides that where national law is sufficient for what the ICC might otherwise do, it takes precedence), it nevertheless impugns the sovereignty of nation states. I answer that a reduction of sovereignty in the appropriate respect and degree is a good thing.

Others object that a process of 'judicial creep' will eventually extend the ICC's powers to competence over, say, drug smuggling, environmental pollution, and beyond. Where, they ask, will it stop? I answer that some of these extensions would be a good thing, given the globalisation of the world economy and the irrevocable interdependence of the world comity. But I reject the implicit 'slippery-slope' argument; it is not beyond the wit of man to see where the jurisdiction of an ICC is most effectively applied, and where not.

Another objection is that the ICC will involve a great deal of cost and bureaucracy. I answer: the solution is, first, to manage it well; and secondly, to accept that peace and justice are worth paying for.

A yet further objection is that the international community will incur vast obligations to compensate the victims of crimes against humanity. A worthy objection, this – for we must certainly at all costs avoid helping survivors of rape, bombing, and ethnic cleansing, must we not?

The Rome Treaty is one of the more hopeful things to have happened in recent years. It is easy to mock endeavours to improve the world – it is a time-honoured and honourable journalistic recreation to knock Big Ideas as a way of testing them – but my guess is that, in a generation or two, the work of the ICC in its then form will bring satisfaction to the hearts of many, and will make your option – which is that nothing but the international equivalent of a punch on the nose will ever be efficacious – seem thoroughly primitive at last.

In the article to which my first letter was a response you dwelt at length on the practical difficulty of making the ICC work, and the related likelihood that its existence will reduce US willingness to police the world. You say that practical concerns are what interest you least; but in fact, although you wish to concentrate (I think rightly) on matters of greater generality, your concerns remain practical nonetheless: for in essence your argument is that there is no such a thing as an 'international community', and therefore only an historically evolved practice of law-governedness in tribal, ethnic or national settings can work. And because there is no 'international community' the assumptions and hopes of human rights advocates are bound to fail, based as they are on what you take to be the false idea that humankind can be holistically viewed as a nation or tribe writ large.

You charge ICC advocates like me with seeking to 'subdue national sovereignty through the back door of international law', and you regard the ICC as undemocratic, and on these grounds suggest that it is not, as I argued, 'morally right to establish an ICC'. Your case, to repeat, is a practical one: you argue that law only works on a national level; that only there can it be democratically accountable; that only there is it the result of the organic evolution which justifies it and makes it suitable to its domain. In refuting these claims, I hope I can convince you that the ICC represents a moral goal after all.

I indeed take the view you repudiate, viz. that mankind is one big (currently unhappy) family, and consider your opposing view about the naturalness of smaller units – the nation, the ethnic group – to be both false and harmful.

First, we live now in a massively globalised and interdependent world. None but the least developed sectors of undeveloped economies is free of international connections. This has been increasingly the case since 1945, and that is why there is now so much effective international law in the commercial and maritime domains. The ICC envisages a far more precisely defined role in the criminal sphere than these; the mere fact of their existence, and their utility, are therefore hopeful signs. Global interdependence and the existence of hundreds of effective international institutions from charities like the Red Cross to UNICEF to the International Court of Justice in the Hague (to say nothing of large treaty organisations like trading blocs and multinational military alliances) shows that supra-national groupings, and by extension the international community itself, are concrete realities. You imply that the feebleness of the UN is evidence to the contrary; but although the UN is indeed paralysed by divisiveness among its members, and drastically hamstrung by lack of funds, it has not long been in existence – and global consciousness is growing fast, as proved by the very fact that the ICC treaty has been signed.

Secondly, the nation state in which you repose faith is an entity with a short and horribly troubled history. Whereas I can understand the concept of humankind (as contrasted, say, to chimpanzee-kind or rabbit-kind), I find the concepts of 'tribe', 'race' and 'nation' peculiarly difficult to grasp, and if graspable, deeply unattractive: I see their logical conclusion in Hitler, and the phrase 'national sovereignty' grates in my ears as '*casus belli*', which it has far too often been. I certainly do not think that state boundaries, almost all drawn on the world map by wars, confer sacred status on the groups of people living within them. The notions smack of racism; nationalism (racism's disguised maiden aunt) is especially fruitful in generating conflicts, even though there is hardly any set of political boundaries anywhere which encloses a racially homogeneous people whose ancestors have tilled their land since Noah.

If you have a point in this connection, it concerns democracy; but the descendants of Germans in Pennsylvania and Frenchmen in Louisiana and Spaniards in California and Englishmen and Dutchmen and Irishmen in New England all have a vote in the same elections in a country as big as all the states of Europe together; so it would seem that large political entities of diverse peoples can be democratic, and I cannot think of any reason to put an upper limit on the numbers involved. (Perhaps you will reply with another practical objection!)

In the past, slowness of communication made political units small. It took time and effort to introduce the rule of law over increasingly large communities, and there were many failures. Those of us who enjoy life in law-abiding communities do well to give thanks for the blessing daily. The ideal of bringing all humanity under a single rule of law, by consent and with mutual aid in making it effective, is admittedly utopian; but as with anything in which the principle is indisputably good, the task should be to strive to approximate it as closely as possible. That is what the ICC represents, and arguments to the effect that only nation-state institutions can work, and that there is no such thing as an international community (no such thing as mankind? no such thing as fellow human beings elsewhere in the world?) ring hollow in comparison.

You rightly insist on looking at realities: so let us look at the world as it actually is. It staggers under a burden of conflicts and inequities. Only a minority of its population – chiefly, we in the comfortable West – live peacefully and flourishingly; but a mere generation ago (in the former Yugoslavia, mere years ago) even we were bombing one another's civilian populations – or rounding them up to 'cleanse' or gas them. And we still have the capacity for global suicide if the recently ended squabbles revive, or the inevitable new ones get out of hand.

Imaginative and courageous minds in Europe, horrified by the bloody results of nationalistic rivalry and racist ideology in the twentieth century, are engaged in trying to forge new international arrangements in our continent, under which its residents are people first and some particular nationality second, and under which each individual has the hope of protection by, or redress against, his fellow humans if he is the victim of wrong from any quarter, internal or external. The arguments for the ICC and other internationalising arrangements generalise this worthy impulse to the world at large.

The aim is to provide everyone on the planet with peaceful, civilised means for preventing or at least lessening conflict and tyranny. I accept that this internationalism – this faith in binding all the world's people together under agreed conceptions of rights and laws – constitutes an ideology. But any view we take about how to organise ourselves, including yours, is construable as such. There is no harm in that; we cannot do without some or other theory. We just have to ensure that it is a good one, and keep it under lively scrutiny.

An ideology, however utopian, which aims at international peace and co-operation under an agreed

JUSTICE AT LAST?   225

rule of law, seems far preferable to me than a nation-state ideology, which is a tried and disastrously failed recipe for competition and conflict, subject to nothing but military power when matters go too far – as they so often do. This ugly state of affairs has been the norm too long, which is why the alternative ideal of a worldwide dispensation of law is so attractive.

I agree with you that there must be democratic controls on the institutions which adopt and administer that law. It is implicit in your view that you think the world too big a place for democracy; so you must think there is an upper limit to how large a law-governed community can be. The USA (a recent – in historical terms – blending of peoples, colonies, currencies, laws) is big; is it too big, or just the right size? When did it become the right size? Will it still work as a democracy (if indeed it works at present, given how few people vote and how much money it takes to be a candidate for elective office) when the population has doubled some decades from now? Or consider China: will democracy always be an impossibility there because of numbers? China has a fifth of the world's population. If it could conceivably be a democracy, why could the world as a whole not be one?

As you see, I think your advocacy of localism against internationalism is motivated by ungroundedly pessimistic practical considerations. I do not think it likely that the world will ever be one country with one government, but that does not mean that its peoples cannot jointly create and operate institutions like the ICC. Indeed it is exactly my point (arguing *ab esse ad posse*) that, to the world's benefit, such institutions already exist, and function effectively, in large numbers: and that this is a growing trend, the trend of the future. Sending large numbers of young men to kill each other as a way of settling disputes seems such a primitive resource in comparison, reminiscent of schoolyard fisticuffs – but with guided missiles and chemical or nuclear warheads. As has been well said, we are cleverer now than when we fought with spears, but not wiser. The ICC and similar institutions are coming into existence because the world cannot afford the old ways any longer, and is therefore trying to grow up and become wise at last.

The foregoing words were written at a moment when the idea of the processes of law embodying protections for human rights and civil liberties had received a boost from the founding of the ICC. That this important event happened as Western states were beginning to reverse some of their hard-won achievements in rights and liberties is an irony; and it exemplifies yet again the fact that history is woven from very mixed threads. But it also reminds us that the fight for freedom of the human individual has to be conducted on all levels, and constantly; if we win it at the level of our individual lives in our societies, there will be no oppressors for the ICC to prosecute, because they will have become impossible.

Appendix 1

Laws and measures that have reduced civil liberties in the United Kingdom and the United States in recent years.

A principal but by no means exclusive driver of reductions on liberties in the UK since 1997 has been the raft of anti-terrorism and associated legislation introduced by the Labour Government:

Terrorism Act 2000
Anti-Terrorism, Crime and Security Act 2001
The Civil Contingencies Act 2004
Prevention of Terrorism Act 2005
Terrorism Act 2006
Identity Cards Act 2006
Counter-Terrorism Act 2008

Other measures that have contributed to the same liberty-diminishing effect include:

Crime and Disorder Act 1998
Criminal Justice (Terrorism and Conspiracy) Act 1998

Regulation of Investigatory Powers Act 2000
Criminal Justice and Police Act 2001
Nationality Immigration and Asylum Act 2002
Anti-Social Behavour Act 2003
Criminal Justice Act 2003
Children Act 2004
Serious Organised Crime and Police Act 2005
Regulation of Investigatory Powers (Communications and
    Data) (Additional Functions and Amendment) Order 2006
UK Borders Act 2007
Tribunals Courts and Enforcement Act 2007

Note that these measures follow more than two decades of legislation for counter-terrorism measures, most of it up to the Terrorism Act 2000 claiming, on first introduction, to be temporary and designed only to provide the security services and courts with capacity to deal with IRA terrorism while the threat lasted. In fact many of the provisions in these measures remain in force, sometimes incorporated into new legislation to give it permanent effect.

The Human Rights Act 1998 (HRA) might be thought a counter to the threat to civil liberties in these instruments, but alas it is a measure of equivocal value because practically every right stated in the Act carries a second clause providing for derogation from it. For example, its important Article 8 protecting privacy is rendered nugatory by the attached derogation, which removes all protection from most of the surveillance powers acquired by government and the security services since the HRA came into force. And the courts have no power to strike down legislation incompatible with the HRA; they can only make a declaration of incompatibility and require the government to review the matter.

The way that attempts to apply the HRA to protect civil liberties in the face of the onslaught of liberty-reducing laws have backfired is illustrated by the following. In 2004 the House of Lords ruled (in *A and Others*) that the Anti-Terrorism Crime and Security Act of 2001 violated human rights by licensing indefinite detention of terrorism suspects, and by discriminating against such suspects on grounds of their nationality and immigration status. The government responded by introducing 'Control Orders' in the Prevention of Terrorism Act 2005 which had the effect of extending powers of detention considerably.

The powers assumed by the government and security services under the measures listed above are as follows:

The **Terrorism Act 2000** broadens the definition of 'terrorism' to cover domestic acts and motivations of religious, political or ideological kinds, and creates a new offence of incitement to terrorism. It gives police extended stop and search powers, and extends the period of detention before charge to seven days. A number of organisations were outlawed as terrorist organisations (including Al-Qaeda; this, note, was before 9/11).

The **Regulation of Investigatory Powers Act 2000** was the first step in extending already existing powers of surveillance relating to covert operations to watch individuals and collect information about them secretly, including taking photographs and video footage, eavesdropping on communications, entering private premises, following, and opening mail. It gives the government powers to oblige internet service providers to fit equipment to enable surveillance of internet users. This Act and the subsequent **Regulation of Investigatory Powers (Communications and Data) (Additional Functions and Amendment) Order 2006** – note the nature of this instrument – bring an end to private communication; all 'private' communication in any form is now open to inspection by government and the security services at their discretion.

The **Anti-Terrorism, Crime and Security Act 2001** enabled

the government to freeze assets of terrorism suspects and gave the Home Secretary powers to detain indefinitely and without charge any foreign national suspected of terrorism. This as noted above was challenged by the House of Lords and has now been replaced by the use of Control Orders. The Act also requires airlines to provide the authorities with information about passengers, banks to inform the authorities of anything suspicious in their customers' activities, and general retention by service providers, for lengthy periods, of their communications data.

The **Criminal Justice Act 2003** increased the length of pre-charge detention of suspects from seven to fourteen days.

The **Children Act 2004**, which came into effect in January 2008, collects and pools information about all children living in England. The information is available to officials but not to parents. It is the starting point for a totalising cache of information on every citizen which will be complete and exhaustive once it is combined with identity card data for adults and collated onto the National identity Register.

The **Civil Contingencies Act 2004** provides that in a situation deemed to be an emergency, any senior minister can issue emergency regulations by Order in Council to protect life, communications, and supplies of money, fuel, water and food. It empowers confiscation of property without compensation, enforced movement of people from one location to another, prohibition of any such movement or travel, enforced labour of citizens, deployment of armed forces, the stipulation of new offences, and the setting up of new courts and tribunals.

The **Prevention of Terrorism Act 2005** introduced the aforementioned Control Orders to enable the authorities to restrict the movements and activities of people suspected of involvement, in some way, in terrorism, while lacking sufficient evidence to charge them.

The **Serious Organised Crime and Police Act 2005** forbids demonstrations within one kilometre of Parliament without police permission. The police can also dictate how many people can take part, and the type of banners (thus: what they say) that can be used.

The **Identity Cards Act 2006** provides that more than fifty items of personal information will be transferred from the control of the individual himself or herself to a National Identity Register maintained by the government and its agencies. A record will be kept of all of an individual's significant transactions through the electronic trail left by use of the ID card to access all goods and services involving interaction with government and with major private agencies such as banks.

The **Terrorism Act 2006** increased the period of pre-charge detention from fourteen to twenty-eight days and outlaws 'glorification of terrorism'.

The **UK Borders Act 2007** gives immigration officers police-like powers of detention, entry, search and seizure.

The **Counter-Terrorism Act 2008** legalises the questioning of individuals already charged under other anti-terrorist legislation, and licenses the police to take fingerprints and DNA swabs from persons subject to Control Orders.

It is clear from these measures what the defender of civil liberties will find objectionable in them. Remember the context: in a setting of ever-increasing surveillance by a variety of means, from CCTV cameras to communications intercepts, these laws change and extend the definition of terrorism, and create a set of instruments which, in all frankness, are more characteristic of what we once called a 'police state' than a liberal democracy, including lengthened periods of detention without charge or trial; stop, search and house-arrest or control powers outside the court system; limitations on the right to protest; limitations on free speech, introduced as restraint on 'support of terrorism' but in principle extendable to any inconvenient or unwanted speech; collection and retention of personal data; and (with proposed forthcoming measures) personal tagging and monitoring of individuals through an identity card scheme linked to a National Identity Register pooling all information about individuals. These measures apply to the population as a whole, any member of which can now fall under one or more provisions of the counter-terrorism legislation on suspicion.

To explore further just one example of the effect on civil liberties of these provisions, consider the matter of Control Orders. These violate the principle enshrined in Magna Carta which in 1215 stated that 'no free man shall be captured, imprisoned, or robbed of his freehold or his liberties … but by the lawful judgment of his peers or by the law of the land'. This has been the chief safeguard of individual liberty (and in fact the only written one) for all the centuries since. If it is argued that the Prevention of Terrorism Act 2005 is 'law of the land' enough for restriction of an individual's liberty on grounds of mere suspicion untested by the courts, then the 2005 Act itself is in violation of the deep principle, and its implications, of *habeas corpus*. The European Convention on Human Rights Article 5 states: 'No arrest or detention unless it is for the purpose of bringing them to court because there is reasonable suspicion they have committed a criminal offence.' Both Control Orders and the extended powers of immigration officials are in violation of this article.

The vital question of the proportionality of these measures arises here: on the basis of 'secret intelligence' which the public cannot by definition assess, the authorities claim justification from the level of terrorist threat for these and other measures. On this ground a cage of invasive and restrictive powers is being erected that turns ordinary citizens into permanent potential suspects under state supervision.

And it is a major concern that the way these powers are arrogated by the state is itself insufficiently under public and democratic control: the extension from fourteen to twenty-eight days detention without charge or trial, was enabled by Parliament under the promise that the new limit was to be employed for one year only; but in the Terrorism Act 2006 the Home Secretary was empowered to continue detaining for twenty-eight days without charge by statutory instrument. Likewise the powers under the Regulation of Investigatory Powers Act have been extended by ministerial order in the Regulation of Investigatory Powers (Communications and Data) (Additional Functions and Amendment) Order 2006, just one example of creeping arrogation of civil-liberty-reducing powers without proper scrutiny or restraint.

This applies even more so to a measure such as the Civil Contingencies Act 2004, which confers dictatorial powers on an individual minister in time of emergency, without provision for objective tests of whether the powers are called for, without appeal from them, and without provision for subsequent audit of and accountability for the exercise of those powers. Indubitably some such powers are appropriate in a time of exceptionally high emergency, but without checks in operation and subsequent audit and accountability – itself always a major check on the exercise of powers – they are a recipe for the full realisation of a *1984* scenario all by themselves.

The effects of anti-terrorism legislation and associated provisions in criminal justice and other legislation is, however, only part of the story. In a wide variety of other and often more insidious ways the government has been dismantling, and continues to dismantle, aspects of the structure of rights and liberties which protect individual citizens. Some examples – it would take too much space to give an exhaustive account – are as follows:

The Children Act 2004, which came into effect in January 2008, collects and pools information about all children living in England. The information is available to officials but not to parents. It is the starting point for a totalising collection of data about all citizens; this with the ID card scheme will eventually mean that individuals are naked to the official gaze in every aspect of their lives, in the interests of monitoring and control. Presumably a utopian aim of ending terrorism and crime by achieving a water-tight surveillance state is what lies behind the long-term project of which the Children Act and ID card scheme are part.

The government is also aiming to achieve immunity for its security-related operations. The Coroners and Justice Bill 2009 will end the independent power of coroners to investigate suspicious deaths and if necessary call government to account over them; an example is the deaths of Iraqis in the British Army sphere in relation to the latter's activities there. The Bill proposes to give the Justice Secretary power to suspend an enquiry, or to order that it be held in secret, under a 'national security' blanket.

It was once the case that an Englishman's home really was his castle; it could not be entered by the authorities without a warrant from a magistrate, duly and properly acquired by the police and lawfully executed by them. The Tribunals Courts and Enforcement Act 2007 has ended the legal sanctity of the private home by empowering bailiffs to enter and distrain goods in recovery of fines imposed by magistrates, and while doing so to restrain individuals within the premises.

Although not included in the list above, it is appropriate to mention that the principle that every accused person has the right to be tried before a jury of his peers has been further eroded by the Domestic Violence, Crime and Victims Act 2004, which provides that the prosecution can apply for trial in the absence of a jury if some of the indictments on the account can by their nature be tried without a jury. The role of juries is to be further limited by the Coroners and Justice Bill 2009 which empowers ministers to order an inquest to be held without a jury.

Civil Liberties in the USA's 'War on Terror':

In the United States the use of warrantless wiretaps has been vigorously opposed by the American Civil Liberties Union and other bodies, both through campaigning and through direct legal action against the government. US civil liberties anxieties have focused on the USA Patriot Act 2001, the draconian proposals embodied in 'Patriot 2' in 2003 (proper title 'Domestic Security Enhancement Act 2003'; it was not enacted as such but various of its provisions have been incorporated in other laws since passed), re-authorisation of the Patriot Act 2005, which made a number of the provisions of the original act permanent and introduced some safeguards – regarding which President George W. Bush said in his signing statement that he would ignore them in the interests of security; he and his administration chose to rely on the view that the US President has virtually unlimited powers in wartime, which is one reason for the state-of-war stance of the Bush administrations since 9/11. John Yoo, then general counsel for the Senate Judiciary Committee and a former clerk for Supreme Court Justice Clarence Thomas, wrote a book-length article for the California Law Review in 1996 arguing that, under the Constitution, a president has far greater powers during wartime than is generally recognised, and that basically Congress then has only two means to restrain a president: by restricting spending, and by impeaching the president. Yoo further claimed that the federal courts have no power over the president in wartime circumstances. Yoo has remained a vocal defender of presidential wartime privilege and more particularly of the actions of the George W. Bush administration in its surveillance activities, and in its detention and torture programme at Guantanamo Bay.

The History Commons website (www.historycommons.org) provides a comprehensive chronological account of the US government's assault on civil liberties and the efforts made to combat it: it is highly recommended. By skimming the headlines of its entries one can see a timeline of the battle for liberties waged in the US during the George W. Bush administrations.

The saga is given in outline below. It is first worth mentioning that FBI and CIA activity in the 1950s and 1960s led to the outbreak of a major controversy in the 1970s and consequently the reining-in of secret surveillance and operations by those agencies. But the continuing need for security soon reasserted itself, and in the years before George W. Bush was elected there were several initiatives that came to be problematic during his presidency. One was that starting in 1997 laws were passed to oblige internet service providers to give government access to networks. The National Security Agency (NSA) 'Trailblazer' Data Mining Program began in 1999. In 2000 the Echelon international data gathering system run by the US raised major concerns over global monitoring of communications; there were several worrying aspects of this, including the fact that Echelon information on businesses in other countries was provided to US corporations, a proceeding that led to a European Parliament protest.

From the time that George W. Bush entered office the assault on civil liberties began to accelerate. It is thought that the 'Groundbreaker' project to monitor domestic telephone communications was set up in February 2001. In that same month the NSA opened discussions with telecommunications firm AT&T on secret monitoring of domestic communications traffic. It also approached other communications companies to ask for domestic phone records and surveillance access; all agreed apart from Qwest, which persistently held out over the coming years to repeated requests and pressure.

According to the History Commons chronology, the FBI escalated warrantless wiretapping of US citizens dramatically, a fact that was not learned by the US public until classified documents fell into the hands of Electronic Privacy Information Centre (EPIC) in October 2005. EPIC is an advocacy group which initiated legal action against the US Justice Department for records relating to the Patriot Act 2001.

In a book by Ronald Kessler entitled *The Terrorist Watch* (Crown, 2007) the NSA launched a domestic surveillance programme two weeks after the 9/11 attacks, amounting to a 'huge' data-mining operation aiming at achieving 'total information awareness' relating to the civil population. The NSA's activities in this respect were not known to the US public until press reports in 2006. This presumably was one of the things Vice President Dick Cheney meant when he stated on 16 September 2001 that the US's response to 9/11 would involve using 'the dark side of intelligence methods'.

John Yoo wrote a legal memo on behalf of the Justice Department in September 2001 authorising warrantless surveillance of international communications.

By October 2001 the NSA had begun its database of US citizens' phone calls, the data being provided by AT&T, BellSouth, Verizon and other companies (but not Qwest). The public were not aware of this until press reports in May 2006.

At this time President George W. Bush's signature was put to a Congressional Resolution authorising the use of force against Iraq; in doing so he described war against Iraq as a 'last resort'.

From 2002 onwards millions, of US citizens were assigned a 'terrorism risk score', again without their knowledge. In the later part of that year AT&T began construction of secret surveillance facilities, closed to all but authorized staff, at its main operations centre.

Congress was informed in December 2002 by Assistant Attorney General William Moschella of the government's possibly illegal use of data-mining electronic surveillance. Moschella justified it on the grounds that the country was facing an emergency.

In 2003, Jack Goldsmith became head of the Office of Legal Council (OLC) in Washington, and immediately began to contest the extent of use of executive powers by the White House. His battle to do so was not to last long, but he began by reviewing the legality of warrantless wiretapping, and by withdrawing the Yoo memos earlier issued by the OLC to authorise torture. Goldsmith also ran into conflict with Cheney's office over the detention of terrorism suspects. While this was happening civil liberties activists and law scholars were contesting the use of National Security Letters (NSLs) which the security services were issuing to get information and compliance from many private bodies and institutions. Among the complaints was the lack of oversight by Congress of NSL use and abuse.

The administration fought back vigorously against all efforts to curb its powers and limit the extent of security measures being taken. Vice President Cheney in particular led the campaign to defend warrantless wiretapping activities. In June 2004, Goldsmith resigned as head of the OLC because of the conflict with the White House.

In 2005, Judge Colleen Kollar-Kotelly, presiding judge of the Foreign Intelligence Surveillance court (FISA), expressed concern that the Justice Department was using evidence gathered by means of warrantless wiretaps, and said that if they continued to do so, FISA would be reluctant to issue warrants in future.

In the summer of 2005 the 'Connecticut Four' sued the Justice Department over an NSL requiring them to turn over private information about all the users of the Connecticut library where one of the Four, George Christian, was librarian. The NSL had been issued because someone had sent a terrorist threat message from one of the library's computers (it turned out to be a hoax), but the NSL demanded information on all library users.

In August 2005, FBI Director George Mueller told InfraGard members that by conducting surveillance on colleagues and employees they were helping the national security effort. InfraGard is an organisation of businessmen and corporate employees who give information to the FBI on matters they regard as suspicious. Mueller urged InfraGard members to tell the FBI about 'disgruntled employees' also.

In October 2005, President George W. Bush signed Executive Order 13388 authorising the FBI to collect data on US citizens without their knowledge, greatly expanding the US government's power to collect and store data on private individuals.

In the autumn of 2005 FISA report that it has learned of more wiretapping warrant applications based on illegally obtained evidence.

On 6 December 2006, President George W. Bush had a conversation with senior *New York Times* personnel asking them to suppress a news story about illegal wiretapping. When this failed he acknowledged, on 17 December, the use of such wiretapping, and accused the press of undermining national security efforts by reporting illegal surveillance.

On 21 December 2005, Judge James Robertson resigned from the FISA court in protest at the warrantless wiretapping programme. The programme is likened in the press to attempts by the South African government during the apartheid years to suppress stories about apartheid.

The Justice Department offered security justifications for use of illegal wiretaps. Discussion of wiretapping reveals that the extent of the NSA surveillance network is far larger than had been supposed; and its work was being facilitated by the National Security Telecommunications Advisory Committee (NSTAC). The ranking Democrat on the House Intelligence Committee, Jane Harman, told the President that his government's practice of keeping most members of Congress ignorant of the surveillance tactics being employed was illegal.

To further government embarrassment, the US Senate learned in early 2006 that the Internal Revenue Service has been collecting party affiliation data on citizens in twenty States of the Union.

As these events unfolded, AT&T was sued for collaborating with the NSA on surveillance; this begins an effort by the government to secure immunity for private companies which have helped the administration in its surveillance activities. It also received a boost from a federal judge asserting that the government is empowered by the Patriot Act to trace email data without warrant. In February 2006, the White House and Congress reached a deal to avoid full hearings on warrantless wiretapping; and in March Bush signed the Patriot Re-Authorisation Act.

This respite for the White House was short-lived. Five former members of the judge's panel on the Foreign Intelligence Surveillance Court jointly spoke out against the use of warrantless wiretaps against citizens of the United States, and urged Congress to give the court powers to monitor the activity of the security services in this respect. They all expressed to the Senate their doubts about the President's powers in ordering surveillance of US citizens without warrant, and that evidence gained by that means is tainted and might be ineffective in court proceedings.

On 9 May 2006, the NSA quashed a Justice Department investigation into the wiretapping programme, but only days later a former NSA analyst, Ira Winkler, went public with his criticism of the NSA's surveillance activities, denouncing it as illegal, against the NSA's rules of engagement, and harmful to its long-term mission.

The legal action against AT&T produced two surprises in late May 2006: the company's lawyers inadvertently released 'redacted' documents pertaining to the case, and the government acted to secure dismissal of the lawsuit on grounds that 'state secrets' were involved. The lawsuit itself alleged unconstitutional behaviour by the administration and its security arms.

Meanwhile, an even more worrying development was afoot: the passage of the Military Commissions Act 2006 (MCA), whose stated purpose is to 'authorise trial by military commission for violations of the law of war, and for other purposes'. The Act elicited a major outcry. One lawyer described it as 'legalising tyranny in the United States', and law professor Marty Lederman argued that the government's claim that the MCA applied only to non-US citizens was incorrect: 'If the Pentagon says you're an unlawful enemy combatant, using whatever criteria they wish, then as far as Congress and US law are concerned, you are one.' On 28 September 2006 Amnesty International joined the condemnation of the law; the *New York Times* stated, 'Rather than reining in the formidable presidential powers Mr Bush and Vice

President Dick Cheney have asserted since September 11, 2001, the law gives some of those powers a solid statutory foundation.'

On 19 October 2006, a swingeing attack on Bush and the MCA and its implications was delivered on air by MSNBC political commentator Keith Olbermann under the heading, 'Beginning the End of America'. By accepting this law, Olbermann said, the nation has accepted that to fight the terrorists, the US government must become 'just a little bit like the terrorists'. But 'the ultimate threat to the nation is not terrorists it is George W. Bush himself': 'We have a long and painful history of ignoring the prophecy attributed to Benjamin Franklin that "those who would give up essential liberty to purchase a little temporary safety, deserve neither liberty nor safety".' Directly addressing Bush, Olbermann continued: 'But even within this history we have not before codified the poisoning of *habeas corpus*, that wellspring of protection from which all essential liberties flow. You, sir, have now befouled that spring. You, sir, have now given us chaos and called it order. You, sir, have now imposed subjugation and called it freedom. For the most vital, the most urgent, the most inescapable of reasons. And – again, Mr Bush – all of them, wrong.' The MCA gives 'a blank check drawn against our freedom to a man [Bush – or any president] who may now, if he so decides, declare not merely any non-American citizens "unlawful enemy combatants" and ship them somewhere – anywhere – but may now, if he so decides, declare you an "unlawful enemy combatant" and ship you somewhere – anywhere'. *Habeas corpus* is now 'gone' for those in the prison camps, and Geneva Conventions protections are 'optional'. Olbermann concluded: 'The moral force we shined outwards to the world as an eternal beacon, and inwards at ourselves as an eternal protection? Snuffed out. These things you have done, Mr Bush, they would be "the beginning of the end of America".'

On 20 October 2006, the government used the MCA to remove detainees from the jurisdiction of the US District Court in Washington, where 196 *habeas corpus* petitions had been filed on behalf of Guantanamo detainees.

On 17 January 2007, US Attorney General Alberto Gonzales provoked a furore by stating before the Senate Judiciary Committee that *habeas corpus* is not protected by the US Constitution. The Senators present did not accept his reading of the Constitution and Gonzales was obliged to modify his statement.

At the beginning of February 2007 government lawyers confirmed that the MCA applied to US citizens also. Because the MCA dispenses with *habeas corpus* the ACLU and others vigorously criticised it.

On 20 July 2007, President George W. Bush signed Executive Order 13440 authorising continued use by the CIA of 'harsh interrogation methods' against terrorism suspects in US custody. On 27 September 2007 a Justice Department official defended the use of 'harsh' methods and claimed that they were in compliance with the Geneva Conventions.

At the beginning of April 2008 the Electronic Frontier Foundation (EFF), which had already taken legal action in connection with surveillance issues, joined with the ACLU to criticise a Justice Department memo stating that the Fourth Amendment, which guards individuals against unreasonable searches and seizures by the authorities, does not apply to government actions against terrorists.

In August 2007 a perceptive article is published by the Director of the Brennan Centre for Justice at New York University, Aziz Huq, who describes the US government as performing a three-step waltz thus: the government suffers a court defeat over some aspect of its security activities; some weeks or months later it announces that the ruling has created a security crisis which immediate legislation must be introduced to remedy; the third step is the legislation being pushed quickly through a compliant Congress, giving even greater powers than were originally contested in the legal action that began the process.

In October 2007, the ACLU published a book detailing the

'systematic' torture of detainees under the authority of the US government. In February 2008 the Pentagon announced its intention to put six alleged 9/11 conspirators on trial, seeking the death penalty for them; and on 27 April 2008, the Justice Department stated that the government has discretion to decide when the Geneva Conventions apply in interrogation. In any case, according to Justice Department letters to Congress, the Geneva Conventions' proscription of treatment that 'outrages personal dignity' does not apply automatically to terrorism suspects.

In the last ten days of January 2009, the newly sworn-in President Barack Obama ordered an end to the Guantanamo trials, banned the use of torture, nullified the legal opinions provided on this matter to the Bush administration, and ordered the closure of the Guantanamo facility.

A concluding comment on the state of civil liberties in the US as a result of the Bush 'War on Terror' might be quoted from an earlier figure, Supreme Court Justice William Brennan, an Eisenhower appointee, who on the basis of his experience as a lawyer and justice wrote that the behaviour of the United States during war is predictable: 'After each perceived security crisis ended, the United States has remorsefully realized that the abrogation of civil liberties was unnecessary. But it has proven unable to prevent itself from repeating the error when the next crisis came along.'

Appendix 2

In this appendix is reprinted the United Nations' Universal Declaration of Human Rights (UDHR), the relevant parts of the European Convention on Human Rights (ECHR) and the United Kingdom's Human Rights Act 1998 (HRA). The latter incorporates the relevant provisions of the former, but it is instructive to note the UK's derogations from the ECHR in the 1980s in connection with the IRA threat, and the implications for the present emergencies and the welfare of the HRA.

2a: The UDHR

Universal Declaration of Human Rights

Preamble

Whereas recognition of the inherent dignity and of the equal and inalienable rights of all members of the human family is the foundation of freedom, justice and peace in the world,

Whereas disregard and contempt for human rights have resulted in barbarous acts which have outraged the conscience of mankind, and the advent of a world in which human beings shall enjoy freedom of speech and belief and freedom from fear and want has been proclaimed as the highest aspiration of the common people,

Whereas it is essential, if man is not to be compelled to have recourse, as a last resort, to rebellion against tyranny and oppression, that human rights should be protected by the rule of law,

Whereas it is essential to promote the development of friendly relations between nations,

Whereas the peoples of the United Nations have in the Charter reaffirmed their faith in fundamental human rights, in the dignity and worth of the human person and in the equal rights of men and women and have determined to promote social progress and better standards of life in larger freedom,

Whereas Member States have pledged themselves to achieve, in co-operation with the United Nations, the promotion of universal respect for and observance of human rights and fundamental freedoms,

Whereas a common understanding of these rights and freedoms is of the greatest importance for the full realization of this pledge,

Now, Therefore, The General Assembly proclaims

This Universal Declaration Of Human Rights

As a common standard of achievement for all peoples and all nations, to the end that every individual and every organ of society, keeping this Declaration constantly in mind, shall strive by teaching and education to promote respect for these rights and freedoms and by progressive measures, national and international, to secure their universal and effective recognition and observance, both among the peoples of Member States themselves and among the peoples of territories under their jurisdiction.

Article 1
All human beings are born free and equal in dignity and rights. They are endowed with reason and conscience and should act towards one another in a spirit of brotherhood.

Article 2

Everyone is entitled to all the rights and freedoms set forth in this Declaration, without distinction of any kind, such as race, colour, sex, language, religion, political or other opinion, national or social origin, property, birth or other status. Furthermore, no distinction shall be made on the basis of the political, jurisdictional or international status of the country or territory to which a person belongs, whether it be independent, trust, non-self-governing or under any other limitation of sovereignty.

Article 3

Everyone has the right to life, liberty and security of person.

Article 4

No one shall be held in slavery or servitude; slavery and the slave trade shall be prohibited in all their forms.

Article 5

No one shall be subjected to torture or to cruel, inhuman or degrading treatment or punishment.

Article 6

Everyone has the right to recognition everywhere as a person before the law.

Article 7

All are equal before the law and are entitled without any discrimination to equal protection of the law. All are entitled to equal protection against any discrimination in violation of this Declaration and against any incitement to such discrimination.

Article 8

Everyone has the right to an effective remedy by the competent national tribunals for acts violating the fundamental rights granted him by the constitution or by law.

Article 9

No one shall be subjected to arbitrary arrest, detention or exile.

Article 10

Everyone is entitled in full equality to a fair and public hearing by an independent and impartial tribunal, in the determination of his rights and obligations and of any criminal charge against him.

Article 11

(1) Everyone charged with a penal offence has the right to be presumed innocent until proved guilty according to law in a public trial at which he has had all the guarantees necessary for his defence.

(2) No one shall be held guilty of any penal offence on account of any act or omission which did not constitute a penal offence, under national or international law, at the time when it was committed. Nor shall a heavier penalty be imposed than the one that was applicable at the time the penal offence was committed.

Article 12

No one shall be subjected to arbitrary interference with his privacy, family, home or correspondence, nor to attacks upon his honour and reputation. Everyone has the right to the protection of the law against such interference or attacks.

Article 13

(1) Everyone has the right to freedom of movement and residence within the borders of each state.

(2) Everyone has the right to leave any country, including his own, and to return to his country.

Article 14

(1) Everyone has the right to seek and to enjoy in other countries asylum from persecution.

(2) This right may not be invoked in the case of prosecutions genuinely arising from non-political crimes or from acts contrary to the purposes and principles of the United Nations.

Article 15

(1) Everyone has the right to a nationality.

(2) No one shall be arbitrarily deprived of his nationality nor denied the right to change his nationality.

Article 16

(1) Men and women of full age, without any limitation due to race, nationality or religion, have the right to marry and to found a family. They are entitled to equal rights as to marriage, during marriage and at its dissolution.

(2) Marriage shall be entered into only with the free and full consent of the intending spouses.

(3) The family is the natural and fundamental group unit of society and is entitled to protection by society and the State.

Article 17

(1) Everyone has the right to own property alone as well as in association with others.

(2) No one shall be arbitrarily deprived of his property.

Article 18

Everyone has the right to freedom of thought, conscience and religion; this right includes freedom to change his religion or belief, and freedom, either alone or in community with others and in public or private, to manifest his religion or belief in teaching, practice, worship and observance.

Article 19

Everyone has the right to freedom of opinion and expression; this right includes freedom to hold opinions without interference and to seek, receive and impart information and ideas through any media and regardless of frontiers.

Article 20

(1) Everyone has the right to freedom of peaceful assembly and association.

(2) No one may be compelled to belong to an association.

Article 21

(1) Everyone has the right to take part in the government of his country, directly or through freely chosen representatives.

(2) Everyone has the right of equal access to public service in his country.

(3) The will of the people shall be the basis of the authority of government; this will shall be expressed in periodic and genuine elections which shall be by universal and equal suffrage and shall be held by secret vote or by equivalent free voting procedures.

Article 22

Everyone, as a member of society, has the right to social security and is entitled to realization, through national effort and international co-operation and in accordance with the organization and resources of each State, of the economic, social and cultural rights indispensable for his dignity and the free development of his personality.

Article 23

(1) Everyone has the right to work, to free choice of employment, to just and favourable conditions of work and to protection against unemployment.

(2) Everyone, without any discrimination, has the right to equal pay for equal work.

(3) Everyone who works has the right to just and favourable remuneration ensuring for himself and his family an existence

worthy of human dignity, and supplemented, if necessary, by other means of social protection.

(4) Everyone has the right to form and to join trade unions for the protection of his interests.

Article 24

Everyone has the right to rest and leisure, including reasonable limitation of working hours and periodic holidays with pay.

Article 25

(1) Everyone has the right to a standard of living adequate for the health and well-being of himself and of his family, including food, clothing, housing and medical care and necessary social services, and the right to security in the event of unemployment, sickness, disability, widowhood, old age or other lack of livelihood in circumstances beyond his control.

(2) Motherhood and childhood are entitled to special care and assistance. All children, whether born in or out of wedlock, shall enjoy the same social protection.

Article 26

(1) Everyone has the right to education. Education shall be free, at least in the elementary and fundamental stages. Elementary education shall be compulsory. Technical and professional education shall be made generally available and higher education shall be equally accessible to all on the basis of merit.

(2) Education shall be directed to the full development of the human personality and to the strengthening of respect for human rights and fundamental freedoms. It shall promote understanding, tolerance and friendship among all nations, racial or religious groups, and shall further the activities of the United Nations for the maintenance of peace.

(3) Parents have a prior right to choose the kind of education that shall be given to their children.

Article 27

(1) Everyone has the right freely to participate in the cultural life of the community, to enjoy the arts and to share in scientific advancement and its benefits.

(2) Everyone has the right to the protection of the moral and material interests resulting from any scientific, literary or artistic production of which he is the author.

Article 28

Everyone is entitled to a social and international order in which the rights and freedoms set forth in this Declaration can be fully realized.

Article 29

(1) Everyone has duties to the community in which alone the free and full development of his personality is possible.

(2) In the exercise of his rights and freedoms, everyone shall be subject only to such limitations as are determined by law solely for the purpose of securing due recognition and respect for the rights and freedoms of others and of meeting the just requirements of morality, public order and the general welfare in a democratic society.

(3) These rights and freedoms may in no case be exercised contrary to the purposes and principles of the United Nations.

Article 30

Nothing in this Declaration may be interpreted as implying for any State, group or person any right to engage in any activity or to perform any act aimed at the destruction of any of the rights and freedoms set forth herein.

2b: Extract from the ECHR as follows:

The European Convention on Human Rights

The Governments signatory hereto, being Members of the Council of Europe,

Considering the Universal Declaration of Human Rights proclaimed by the General Assembly of the United Nations on 10 December 1948;

Considering that this Declaration aims at securing the universal and effective recognition and observance of the Rights therein declared;

Considering that the aim of the Council of Europe is the achievement of greater unity between its Members and that one of the methods by which the aim is to be pursued is the maintenance and further realization of Human Rights and Fundamental Freedoms;

Reaffirming their profound belief in those Fundamental Freedoms which are the foundation of justice and peace in the world and are best maintained on the one hand by an effective political democracy and on the other by a common understanding and observance of the Human Rights upon which they depend;

Being resolved, as the Governments of European countries which are like-minded and have a common heritage of political traditions, ideals, freedom and the rule of law to take the first steps for the collective enforcement of certain of the Rights stated in the Universal Declaration;

Have agreed as follows:

Article 1
The High Contracting Parties shall secure to everyone within their jurisdiction the rights and freedoms defined in Section I of this Convention.

Section I

Article 2

1. Everyone's right to life shall be protected by law. No one shall be deprived of his life intentionally save in the execution of a sentence of a court following his conviction of a crime for which this penalty is provided by law.

2. Deprivation of life shall not be regarded as inflicted in contravention of this article when it results from the use of force which is no more than absolutely necessary:

(a) in defence of any person from unlawful violence;

(b) in order to effect a lawful arrest or to prevent escape of a person lawfully detained;

(c) in action lawfully taken for the purpose of quelling a riot or insurrection.

Article 3

No one shall be subjected to torture or to inhuman or degrading treatment or punishment.

Article 4

1. No one shall be held in slavery or servitude.

2. No one shall be required to perform forced or compulsory labour.

3. For the purpose of this article the term 'forced or compulsory labour' shall not include:

(a) any work required to be done in the ordinary course of detention imposed according to the provisions of Article 5 of this Convention or during conditional release from such detention;

(b) any service of a military character or, in case of conscientious objectors in countries where they are recognized, service exacted instead of compulsory military service;

(c) any service exacted in case of an emergency or calamity threatening the life or well-being of the community;

(d) any work or service which forms part of normal civic obligations.

Article 5

1. Everyone has the right to liberty and security of person. No one shall be deprived of his liberty save in the following cases and in accordance with a procedure prescribed by law:

(a) the lawful detention of a person after conviction by a competent court;

(b) the lawful arrest or detention of a person for non-compliance with the lawful order of a court or in order to secure the fulfilment of any obligation prescribed by law;

(c) the lawful arrest or detention of a person effected for the purpose on bringing him before the competent legal authority on reasonable suspicion of having committed an offence or when it is reasonably considered necessary to prevent his committing an offence or fleeing after having done so;

(d) the detention of a minor by lawful order for the purpose of educational supervision or his lawful detention for the purpose of bringing him before the competent legal authority;

(e) the lawful detention of persons for the prevention of the spreading of infectious diseases, of persons of unsound mind, alcoholics or drug addicts, or vagrants;

(f) the lawful arrest or detention of a person to prevent his effecting an unauthorized entry into the country or of a person against whom action is being taken with a view to deportation or extradition.

2. Everyone who is arrested shall be informed promptly, in a language which he understands, of the reasons for his arrest and the charge against him.

3. Everyone arrested or detained in accordance with the provisions of paragraph 1(c) of this article shall be brought promptly before a judge or other officer authorized by law to exercise

judicial power and shall be entitled to trial within a reasonable time or to release pending trial. Release may be conditioned by guarantees to appear for trial.

4. Everyone who is deprived of his liberty by arrest or detention shall be entitled to take proceedings by which the lawfulness of his detention shall be decided speedily by a court and his release ordered if the detention is not lawful.

5. Everyone who has been the victim of arrest or detention in contravention of the provisions of this article shall have an enforceable right to compensation.

Article 6

1. In the determination of his civil rights and obligations or of any criminal charge against him, everyone is entitled to a fair and public hearing within a reasonable time by an independent and impartial tribunal established by law. Judgement shall be pronounced publicly but the press and public may be excluded from all or part of the trial in the interest of morals, public order or national security in a democratic society, where the interests of juveniles or the protection of the private life of the parties so require, or to the extent strictly necessary in the opinion of the court in special circumstances where publicity would prejudice the interests of justice.

2. Everyone charged with a criminal offence shall be presumed innocent until proved guilty according to law.

3. Everyone charged with a criminal offence has the following minimum rights:

(a) to be informed promptly, in a language which he understands and in detail, of the nature and cause of the accusation against him;

(b) to have adequate time and the facilities for the preparation of his defence;

(c) to defend himself in person or through legal assistance of his own choosing or, if he has not sufficient means to pay for legal assistance, to be given it free when the interests of justice so require;

(d) to examine or have examined witnesses against him and to obtain the attendance and examination of witnesses on his behalf under the same conditions as witnesses against him;

(e) to have the free assistance of an interpreter if he cannot understand or speak the language used in court.

Article 7

1. No one shall be held guilty of any criminal offence on account of any act or omission which did not constitute a criminal offence under national or international law at the time when it was committed. Nor shall a heavier penalty be imposed than the one that was applicable at the time the criminal offence was committed.

2. This article shall not prejudice the trial and punishment of any person for any act or omission which, at the time when it was committed, was criminal according to the general principles of law recognized by civilized nations.

Article 8

1. Everyone has the right to respect for his private and family life, his home and his correspondence.

2. There shall be no interference by a public authority with the exercise of this right except such as is in accordance with the law and is necessary in a democratic society in the interests of national security, public safety or the economic well-being of the country, for the prevention of disorder or crime, for the protection of health or morals, or for the protection of the rights and freedoms of others.

Article 9

1. Everyone has the right to freedom of thought, conscience and religion; this right includes freedom to change his religion or belief, and freedom, either alone or in community with others and in public or private, to manifest his religion or belief, in worship, teaching, practice and observance.

2. Freedom to manifest one's religion or beliefs shall be subject only to such limitations as are prescribed by law and are necessary in a democratic society in the interests of public safety, for the protection of public order, health or morals, or the protection of the rights and freedoms of others.

Article 10

1. Everyone has the right to freedom of expression. This right shall include freedom to hold opinions and to receive and impart information and ideas without interference by public authority and regardless of frontiers. This article shall not prevent States from requiring the licensing of broadcasting, television or cinema enterprises.

2. The exercise of these freedoms, since it carries with it duties and responsibilities, may be subject to such formalities, conditions, restrictions or penalties as are prescribed by law and are necessary in a democratic society, in the interests of national security, territorial integrity or public safety, for the prevention of disorder or crime, for the protection of health or morals, for the protection of the reputation or the rights of others, for preventing the disclosure of information received in confidence, or for maintaining the authority and impartiality of the judiciary.

Article 11

1. Everyone has the right to freedom of peaceful assembly and to freedom of association with others, including the right to form and to join trade unions for the protection of his interests.

2. No restrictions shall be placed on the exercise of these rights other than such as are prescribed by law and are necessary in a democratic society in the interests of national security or public safety, for the prevention of disorder or crime, for the protection of health or morals or for the protection of the rights and freedoms of others. this article shall not prevent

the imposition of lawful restrictions on the exercise of these rights by members of the armed forces, of the police or of the administration of the State.

Article 12
Men and women of marriageable age have the right to marry and to found a family, according to the national laws governing the exercise of this right.

Article 13
Everyone whose rights and freedoms as set forth in this Convention are violated shall have an effective remedy before a national authority notwithstanding that the violation has been committed by persons acting in an official capacity.

Article 14
The enjoyment of the rights and freedoms set forth in this Convention shall be secured without discrimination on any ground such as sex, race, colour, language, religion, political or other opinion, national or social origin, association with a national minority, property, birth or other status.

Article 15
1. In time of war or other public emergency threatening the life of the nation any High Contracting Party may take measures derogating from its obligations under this Convention to the extent strictly required by the exigencies of the situation, provided that such measures are not inconsistent with its other obligations under international law.
2. No derogation from Article 2, except in respect of deaths resulting from lawful acts of war, or from Articles 3, 4 (paragraph 1) and 7 shall be made under this provision.
3. Any High Contracting Party availing itself of this right of derogation shall keep the Secretary General of the Council of

Europe fully informed of the measures which it has taken and the reasons therefor. It shall also inform the Secretary General of the Council of Europe when such measures have ceased to operate and the provisions of the Convention are again being fully executed.

Article 16

Nothing in Articles 10, 11, and 14 shall be regarded as preventing the High Contracting Parties from imposing restrictions on the political activity of aliens.

Article 17

Nothing in this Convention may be interpreted as implying for any State, group or person any right to engage in any activity or perform any act aimed at the destruction on any of the rights and freedoms set forth herein or at their limitation to a greater extent than is provided for in the Convention.

Article 18

The restrictions permitted under this Convention to the said rights and freedoms shall not be applied for any purpose other than those for which they have been prescribed.

2c: Extract from the HRA as follows:

The Human Rights Act

Part I: The Convention on Rights and Freedoms

Article 2: Right to life

1. Everyone's right to life shall be protected by law. No one shall be deprived of his life intentionally save in the execution of a sentence of a court following his conviction of a crime for which this penalty is provided by law.

APPENDIX 2 261

2. Deprivation of life shall not be regarded as inflicted in contravention of this Article when it results from the use of force which is no more than absolutely necessary:

(a) in defence of any person from unlawful violence;

(b) in order to effect a lawful arrest or to prevent the escape of a person lawfully detained;

(c) in action lawfully taken for the purpose of quelling a riot or insurrection.

Article 3: Prohibition of torture

No one shall be subjected to torture or to inhuman or degrading treatment or punishment.

Article 4: Prohibition of slavery and forced labour

1. No one shall be held in slavery or servitude.

2. No one shall be required to perform forced or compulsory labour.

3. For the purpose of this Article the term 'forced or compulsory labour' shall not include:

(a) any work required to be done in the ordinary course of detention imposed according to the provisions of Article 5 of this Convention or during conditional release from such detention;

(b) any service of a military character or, in case of conscientious objectors in countries where they are recognised, service exacted instead of compulsory military service;

(c) any service exacted in case of an emergency or calamity threatening the life or well-being of the community;

(d) any work or service which forms part of normal civic obligations.

Article 5: Right to liberty and security

1. Everyone has the right to liberty and security of person. No one shall be deprived of his liberty save in the following cases and in accordance with a procedure prescribed by law:

(a) the lawful detention of a person after conviction by a competent court;

(b) the lawful arrest or detention of a person for non-compliance with the lawful order of a court or in order to secure the fulfilment of any obligation prescribed by law;

(c) the lawful arrest or detention of a person effected for the purpose of bringing him before the competent legal authority on reasonable suspicion of having committed an offence or when it is reasonably considered necessary to prevent his committing an offence or fleeing after having done so;

(d) the detention of a minor by lawful order for the purpose of educational supervision or his lawful detention for the purpose of bringing him before the competent legal authority;

(e) the lawful detention of persons for the prevention of the spreading of infectious diseases, of persons of unsound mind, alcoholics or drug addicts or vagrants;

(f) the lawful arrest or detention of a person to prevent his effecting an unauthorised entry into the country or of a person against whom action is being taken with a view to deportation or extradition.

2. Everyone who is arrested shall be informed promptly, in a language which he understands, of the reasons for his arrest and of any charge against him.

3. Everyone arrested or detained in accordance with the provisions of paragraph 1(c) of this Article shall be brought promptly before a judge or other officer authorised by law to exercise judicial power and shall be entitled to trial within a reasonable time or to release pending trial. Release may be conditioned by guarantees to appear for trial.

4. Everyone who is deprived of his liberty by arrest or detention shall be entitled to take proceedings by which the lawfulness of his detention shall be decided speedily by a court and his release ordered if the detention is not lawful.

5. Everyone who has been the victim of arrest or detention in

contravention of the provisions of this Article shall have an enforceable right to compensation.

Article 6: Right to a fair trial

1. In the determination of his civil rights and obligations or of any criminal charge against him, everyone is entitled to a fair and public hearing within a reasonable time by an independent and impartial tribunal established by law. Judgment shall be pronounced publicly but the press and public may be excluded from all or part of the trial in the interest of morals, public order or national security in a democratic society, where the interests of juveniles or the protection of the private life of the parties so require, or to the extent strictly necessary in the opinion of the court in special circumstances where publicity would prejudice the interests of justice.

2. Everyone charged with a criminal offence shall be presumed innocent until proved guilty according to law.

3. Everyone charged with a criminal offence has the following minimum rights:

   (a) to be informed promptly, in a language which he understands and in detail, of the nature and cause of the accusation against him;

   (b) to have adequate time and facilities for the preparation of his defence;

   (c) to defend himself in person or through legal assistance of his own choosing or, if he has not sufficient means to pay for legal assistance, to be given it free when the interests of justice so require;

   (d) to examine or have examined witnesses against him and to obtain the attendance and examination of witnesses on his behalf under the same conditions as witnesses against him;

   (e) to have the free assistance of an interpreter if he cannot understand or speak the language used in court.

Article 7: No punishment without law

1. No one shall be held guilty of any criminal offence on account of any act or omission which did not constitute a criminal offence under national or international law at the time when it was committed. Nor shall a heavier penalty be imposed than the one that was applicable at the time the criminal offence was committed.

2. This Article shall not prejudice the trial and punishment of any person for any act or omission which, at the time when it was committed, was criminal according to the general principles of law recognised by civilised nations.

Article 8: Right to respect for private and family life

1. Everyone has the right to respect for his private and family life, his home and his correspondence.

2. There shall be no interference by a public authority with the exercise of this right except such as is in accordance with the law and is necessary in a democratic society in the interests of national security, public safety or the economic well-being of the country, for the prevention of disorder or crime, for the protection of health or morals, or for the protection of the rights and freedoms of others.

Article 9: Freedom of thought, conscience and religion

1. Everyone has the right to freedom of thought, conscience and religion; this right includes freedom to change his religion or belief and freedom, either alone or in community with others and in public or private, to manifest his religion or belief, in worship, teaching, practice and observance.

2. Freedom to manifest one's religion or beliefs shall be subject only to such limitations as are prescribed by law and are necessary in a democratic society in the interests of public safety, for the protection of public order, health or morals, or for the protection of the rights and freedoms of others.

Article 10: Freedom of expression

1. Everyone has the right to freedom of expression. This right shall include freedom to hold opinions and to receive and impart information and ideas without interference by public authority and regardless of frontiers. This Article shall not prevent States from requiring the licensing of broadcasting, television or cinema enterprises.

2. The exercise of these freedoms, since it carries with it duties and responsibilities, may be subject to such formalities, conditions, restrictions or penalties as are prescribed by law and are necessary in a democratic society, in the interests of national security, territorial integrity or public safety, for the prevention of disorder or crime, for the protection of health or morals, for the protection of the reputation or rights of others, for preventing the disclosure of information received in confidence, or for maintaining the authority and impartiality of the judiciary.

Article 11: Freedom of assembly and association

1. Everyone has the right to freedom of peaceful assembly and to freedom of association with others, including the right to form and to join trade unions for the protection of his interests.

2. No restrictions shall be placed on the exercise of these rights other than such as are prescribed by law and are necessary in a democratic society in the interests of national security or public safety, for the prevention of disorder or crime, for the protection of health or morals or for the protection of the rights and freedoms of others. This Article shall not prevent the imposition of lawful restrictions on the exercise of these rights by members of the armed forces, of the police or of the administration of the State.

Article 12: Right to marry

Men and women of marriageable age have the right to marry and to found a family, according to the national laws governing the exercise of this right.

Article 14: Prohibition of discrimination
The enjoyment of the rights and freedoms set forth in this Convention shall be secured without discrimination on any ground such as sex, race, colour, language, religion, political or other opinion, national or social origin, association with a national minority, property, birth or other status.

Article 16: Restrictions on political activity of aliens
Nothing in Articles 10, 11 and 14 shall be regarded as preventing the High Contracting Parties from imposing restrictions on the political activity of aliens.

Article 17: Prohibition of abuse of rights
Nothing in this Convention may be interpreted as implying for any State, group or person any right to engage in any activity or perform any act aimed at the destruction of any of the rights and freedoms set forth herein or at their limitation to a greater extent than is provided for in the Convention.

Article 18: Limitation on use of restrictions on rights
The restrictions permitted under this Convention to the said rights and freedoms shall not be applied for any purpose other than those for which they have been prescribed.

Part II: The First Protocol

Article 1: Protection of property
Every natural or legal person is entitled to the peaceful enjoyment of his possessions. No one shall be deprived of his possessions except in the public interest and subject to the conditions provided for by law and by the general principles of international law.

The preceding provisions shall not, however, in any way impair the right of a State to enforce such laws as it deems necessary to control the use of property in accordance with the general interest or to secure the payment of taxes or other contributions or penalties.

Article 2: Right to education

No person shall be denied the right to education. In the exercise of any functions which it assumes in relation to education and to teaching, the State shall respect the right of parents to ensure such education and teaching in conformity with their own religious and philosophical convictions.

Article 3: Right to free elections

The High Contracting Parties undertake to hold free elections at reasonable intervals by secret ballot, under conditions which will ensure the free expression of the opinion of the people in the choice of the legislature.

Part III: The Sixth Protocol

Article 1: Abolition of the death penalty

The death penalty shall be abolished. No one shall be condemned to such penalty or executed.

Article 2: Death penalty in time of war

A State may make provision in its law for the death penalty in respect of acts committed in time of war or of imminent threat of war; such penalty shall be applied only in the instances laid down in the law and in accordance with its provisions. The State shall communicate to the Secretary General of the Council of Europe the relevant provisions of that law.

SCHEDULE 3 DEROGATION AND RESERVATION

Part I : Derogation
The 1988 *notification*

The United Kingdom Permanent Representative to the Council of Europe presents his compliments to the Secretary General of the Council, and has the honour to convey the following information in order to ensure compliance with the obligations of Her Majesty's Government in the United Kingdom under Article 15(3) of the Convention for the Protection of Human Rights and Fundamental Freedoms signed at Rome on 4 November 1950.

There have been in the United Kingdom in recent years campaigns of organised terrorism connected with the affairs of Northern Ireland which have manifested themselves in activities which have included repeated murder, attempted murder, maiming, intimidation and violent civil disturbance and in bombing and fire raising which have resulted in death, injury and widespread destruction of property. As a result, a public emergency within the meaning of Article 15(1) of the Convention exists in the United Kingdom.

The Government found it necessary in 1974 to introduce and since then, in cases concerning persons reasonably suspected of involvement in terrorism connected with the affairs of Northern Ireland, or of certain offences under the legislation, who have been detained for 48 hours, to exercise powers enabling further detention without charge, for periods of up to five days, on the authority of the Secretary of State. These powers are at present to be found in Section 12 of the Prevention of Terrorism (Temporary Provisions) Act 1984, Article 9 of the Prevention of Terrorism (Supplemental Temporary Provisions) Order 1984 and Article 10 of the Prevention of Terrorism (Supplemental Temporary Provisions) (Northern Ireland) Order 1984.

Section 12 of the Prevention of Terrorism (Temporary Provisions) Act 1984 provides for a person whom a constable has

arrested on reasonable grounds of suspecting him to be guilty of
an offence under Section 1, 9 or 10 of the Act, or to be or to have
been involved in terrorism connected with the affairs of Northern
Ireland, to be detained in right of the arrest for up to 48 hours
and thereafter, where the Secretary of State extends the detention
period, for up to a further five days. Section 12 substantially re-
enacted Section 12 of the Prevention of Terrorism (Temporary
Provisions) Act 1976 which, in turn, substantially re-enacted
Section 7 of the Prevention of Terrorism (Temporary Provisions)
Act 1974.

Article 10 of the Prevention of Terrorism (Supplemental
Temporary Provisions) (Northern Ireland) Order 1984 (SI
1984/417) and Article 9 of the Prevention of Terrorism
(Supplemental Temporary Provisions) Order 1984 (SI 1984/418)
were both made under Sections 13 and 14 of and Schedule 3 to
the 1984 Act and substantially re-enacted powers of detention in
Orders made under the 1974 and 1976 Acts. A person who is being
examined under Article 4 of either Order on his arrival in, or on
seeking to leave, Northern Ireland or Great Britain for the purpose
of determining whether he is or has been involved in terrorism
connected with the affairs of Northern Ireland, or whether there
are grounds for suspecting that he has committed an offence under
Section 9 of the 1984 Act, may be detained under Article 9 or 10,
as appropriate, pending the conclusion of his examination. The
period of this examination may exceed 12 hours if an examining
officer has reasonable grounds for suspecting him to be or to have
been involved in acts of terrorism connected with the affairs of
Northern Ireland.

Where such a person is detained under the said Article 9 or
10 he may be detained for up to 48 hours on the authority of
an examining officer and thereafter, where the Secretary of State
extends the detention period, for up to a further five days.

In its judgment of 29 November 1988 in the Case of *Brogan and
Others*, the European Court of Human Rights held that there had

been a violation of Article 5(3) in respect of each of the applicants, all of whom had been detained under Section 12 of the 1984 Act. The Court held that even the shortest of the four periods of detention concerned, namely four days and six hours, fell outside the constraints as to time permitted by the first part of Article 5(3). In addition, the Court held that there had been a violation of Article 5(5) in the case of each applicant.

Following this judgment, the Secretary of State for the Home Department informed Parliament on 6 December 1988 that, against the background of the terrorist campaign, and the over-riding need to bring terrorists to justice, the Government did not believe that the maximum period of detention should be reduced. He informed Parliament that the Government were examining the matter with a view to responding to the judgment. On 22 December 1988, the Secretary of State further informed Parliament that it remained the Government's wish, if it could be achieved, to find a judicial process under which extended detention might be reviewed and where appropriate authorised by a judge or other judicial officer. But a further period of reflection and consultation was necessary before the Government could bring forward a firm and final view.

Since the judgment of 29 November 1988 as well as previously, the Government have found it necessary to continue to exercise, in relation to terrorism connected with the affairs of Northern Ireland, the powers described above enabling further detention without charge for periods of up to 5 days, on the authority of the Secretary of State, to the extent strictly required by the exigencies of the situation to enable necessary enquiries and investigations properly to be completed in order to decide whether criminal proceedings should be instituted. To the extent that the exercise of these powers may be inconsistent with the obligations imposed by the Convention the Government has availed itself of the right of derogation conferred by Article 15(1) of the Convention and will continue to do so until further notice.

Dated 23 December 1988.

The 1989 *notification*

The United Kingdom Permanent Representative to the Council of Europe presents his compliments to the Secretary General of the Council, and has the honour to convey the following information.

In his communication to the Secretary General of 23 December 1988, reference was made to the introduction and exercise of certain powers under section 12 of the Prevention of Terrorism (Temporary Provisions) Act 1984, Article 9 of the Prevention of Terrorism (Supplemental Temporary Provisions) Order 1984 and Article 10 of the Prevention of Terrorism (Supplemental Temporary Provisions) (Northern Ireland) Order 1984.

These provisions have been replaced by section 14 of and paragraph 6 of Schedule 5 to the Prevention of Terrorism (Temporary Provisions) Act 1989, which make comparable provision. They came into force on 22 March 1989. A copy of these provisions is enclosed.

The United Kingdom Permanent Representative avails himself of this opportunity to renew to the Secretary General the assurance of his highest consideration.

23 March 1989.

Index

A NOTE ON THE TYPE

The text of this book is set in Bembo. This type was first used in 1495 by the Venetian printer Aldus Manutius for Cardinal Bembo's De Aetna, and was cut for Manutius by Francesco Griffo. It was one of the types used by Claude Garamond (1480–1561) as a model for his Romain de L'Universitë, and so it was the forerunner of what became standard European type for the following two centuries. Its modern form follows the original types and was designed for Monotype in 1929.